THE MINDFUL
MANAGER

THE MINDFUL
MANAGER

THE GOD FACTOR AT WORK

PATRICIA WILSON

FRESH AIR BOOKS®
Nashville

THE MINDFUL MANAGER: THE GOD FACTOR AT WORK
Copyright © 2009 by Patricia Wilson
All rights reserved.

Fresh Air Books Web site: www.freshairbooks.org

FRESH AIR BOOKS® and design logos are trademarks owned by The Upper Room®, a ministry of GBOD®, Nashville, Tennessee. All rights reserved.

Unless otherwise noted, scripture quotations are from the New Revised Standard Version Bible, copyright 1989, Division of Christian Education of the National Council of the Churches of Christ in the United States of America. Used by permission. All rights reserved.

Scripture quotations marked NIV are taken from the HOLY BIBLE, NEW INTERNATIONAL VERSION®. NIV®. Copyright © 1973, 1978, 1984 by International Bible Society. Used by permission of Zondervan. All rights reserved.

Cover images: iStockphotos.com
Cover design: Left Coast Design, Portland, OR / www.lcoast.com
Interior design: Buckinghorse Design / www.buckinghorsedesign.com
First printing: 2009

Library of Congress Cataloging-in-Publication Data
Wilson, Patricia, 1943–
    Mindful manager : the God factor at work / Patricia Wilson.
        p. cm.
    ISBN 978-1-935205-05-0
    1. Businesspeople—Religious life. 2. Business—Religious aspects—Christianity.
3. Leadership—Religious aspects—Christianity. 4. Work—Religious aspects—
Christianity. I. Title.
    BV4596.B8W45 2009
    248.8'8—dc22

2008054065

Printed in the United States of America

This book is dedicated to
all who struggle to
bring the substance of their faith
into the reality of their workplace.

CONTENTS

PART ONE

STARTING WITH YOU

HAVE YOU EVER WONDERED what it would be like to do your job as if you had all the power and resources you'd ever need at your fingertips? Perhaps you often feel that you could be much more effective as a manager if only you could find some kind of magic manager potion. Or perhaps you've struggled with the notion that you really aren't managerial material, and it is only a matter of time before the rest of the world—that is, your employees and your bosses—finds out.

Imagine that you've always wanted to build your own house. To accomplish this, you pursue a number of things to learn about building a house. You attend seminars on house building; you watch carpenters at work on a house; you take lessons in power tool use. Once you have all the information you need to build a house, you acquire land, draw up blueprints, order lumber, and purchase tools. At this moment, you have the power to build the house because you possess the knowledge, the materials, and the tools you need. But the house won't be built until you empower yourself to start building.

In the same way, you must empower yourself before you can begin to access the tools and techniques available to a mindful manager. To do this you must:

1. Become aware of any value conflicts related to your management position that prevent you from expressing your own personal values within your workplace.
2. Find a vision for the job you do. When you have a compelling vision of what you want your work life to be, you can begin to create that vision where you are today.
3. Build your own internal power so that in all circumstances, you can manage mindfully and rely on God in your day-to-day challenges.

1

RECOGNIZING AND DISCOVERING YOUR VALUES IN THE WORKPLACE

Some people enjoy the voyage of self-discovery; others don't. However, from both points of view, self-discovery is a key element in the process of becoming a mindful manager—or even a better manager. Before you can begin to deal with the issues of your workplace—the people, the challenges, the duties, and the deadlines—you need to discover and acknowledge your own strengths, limitations, values, goals, and beliefs. This information becomes a framework upon which you can build your managerial skills. What goes on inside your head can affect what happens on the outside. Your actions and decisions are often determined by your personal biases and beliefs. Everything from how you view your own worth to what you value in your life can either strengthen or weaken your managerial ability. More importantly, knowing what is happening on the inside gives you an impetus to seek God in your workplace—to become mindful.

Did you know that your first thought often is your last thought, and your last thought is your first thought? In other words, if your first thought in the morning is about the job, probably your last thought at night is of that same job. If those thoughts are negative, then you begin and end your day on a negative note. You may find your thoughts consumed with the reorganization of your department and the extra work it will bring you. Or you may continually think about a difficult person you supervise. Or you may be trying to deal with the demands of your position, your boss, and your employees. Even if your thoughts aren't always negative but still relate to your job, you may find that your job is beginning to take over your life.

How can your job consume your life, often to the exclusion of all else? You actually work more than eight hours a day. Most managers do. You may never take a vacation unless it is mandatory. You don't use sick days—you can't afford the luxury of being sick. And you work on most holidays just to get caught up. It is the work that you take home with you—not in your briefcase but in your head—that makes it seem as if every waking minute of your life is spent on the job.

How does a place where you spend only a portion of your time consume so much of your mind and energy? For some, it may simply be a case of workaholism. For others, it is a genuine passion for their jobs. But for the majority of people, the job is work, and all else is subordinate to it.

Is your job becoming such a burden that it affects every other aspect of your life? Check these warning signs and wake-up calls to determine how much your management position is costing you.

Seven Warning Signs and Wake-Up Calls for Managers

1. Making No Difference
Does it seem that nothing ever changes—the difficult tasks, the lazy subordinate, the employee with the bad attitude, or the critical person in the

next office—regardless of what you do, how hard you try, or how much you pray? You may have been fighting the same uphill battle for a long time, yet even after weeks, months, and sometimes years of effort, the hill is just as high. You've tried being nice; you've tried being assertive; you've even tried ignoring the issues. But as your head hits the pillow at night, you're still thinking about that difficult person or situation, mulling over the day's encounters, rethinking what you should have said or should have done. And the next morning, you're thinking about facing the day and the same situation.

2. Waiting Until

Are you like Sleeping Beauty, living in a state of limbo, waiting until her prince comes to wake her up? It's easy to opt out of being engaged in the workplace if you decide that you'll simply mark time until:

> your negative employee retires . . .
> you get that promotion . . .
> the organization is restructured . . .
> you get transferred to another section . . .
> your kids get out of college . . .
> your spouse gets that degree . . .
> you get that degree . . .
> you find another job . . .
> you can retire . . .
> you win the lottery.

If you find that you're not engaged in your workplace, that you hold back from getting involved with others, and that you spend a lot of your time thinking ahead to some future event that will free you from your current situation, then you're in the "waiting until" mode.

3. Not Walking the Talk

Do you find it hard to walk your talk? You may find yourself agreeing with policies and decisions you don't want to implement, giving your employees the "company line," making promises you have no intention of keeping, or going along with the majority. Yet when it comes to crunch time and you have to act on your words, do you find yourself dragging your feet?

At your heart, you consider yourself a person of faith, but is it hard to walk that talk too? Perhaps you find it hard to believe that your faith has any relevance in the workplace.

4. Attitude Shifts

Some mornings you wake up and you can't wait to get to work. You're looking forward to supervising that new project or conducting that staff meeting. Everything seems possible and you're feeling strong and empowered. By the time you get to work, however, you wish you were someone else, somewhere else, doing something else. You've gone from positive to negative in a split second, or in the time it takes for the elevator to get to your floor. You can't believe that the funk you're in is how life is intended to be, yet getting back to an even emotional keel seems impossible.

5. Avoidance

Do you find yourself avoiding certain people, situations, or subjects at work? Perhaps you've changed your lunch hour so you can't be buttonholed by that employee with all the personal problems. Maybe you've asked to be removed from a committee where you find the people difficult to work with. Or you may stay away from social situations at work—refusing invitations to lunch, office parties, or group activities.

Are there subjects you won't talk about? The proposed changes in the organization, the policies of upper management, the problems with the accounting program, the conflict between two of your employees—they're all off-limits with you because you don't want to have to face them or deal with them.

6. Hating Politics

You'd love your job if only it weren't so political in your workplace. Everyone seems to have a hidden agenda, and you're aware of covert alliances, power plays, and dominance struggles. You try not to get involved, hoping that you can sit on the fence and avoid entanglement in the office politics. Most days, you feel as if you're walking on a tightrope in your efforts not to be seen as playing partisan politics. You keep telling yourself that you're above playing politics.

7. Lost Enthusiasm

Are you surviving five to live for two? That is, surviving those five days from Monday to Friday so you can live for the two days of the weekend before survival starts all over again? Does your week go something like this?

Oh no, it's Monday.
Only Tuesday? The week will never end.
Wednesday. Halfway there.
Thursday. Only one more day to go.
Thank God, it's Friday.
Yay! Saturday.
Sunday. Last day before it's back to the grind. Sigh.

Sad, isn't it? So much time spent just surviving. Surely life is meant to be better than this.

These warning signs and wake-up calls tell you that you're losing the meaning and purpose of your workday. Often they're the first symptoms of a dichotomy between your values and motivation on the job, and the values and motivation of the people you work with or the values and motivation of the organization itself.

VALUE CONFLICTS IN THE WORKPLACE

What are your personal values and work motivations? Take the following quiz to determine what is truly important to you.

Directions: In each section, rank the top five things that are important to you. Don't agonize over your responses because there are no right or wrong answers. Instead, do the self-test quickly, going with your first spontaneous choices.

A. What is important to you in life generally? Mark the five items in this list that matter most to you.

```
_____  1. Integrity—my own and that of others
___×____  2. Excelling in whatever I do
_____  3. Power and influence
_____  4. Time to myself
___×____  5. Family
_____  6. Meaningful work
_____  7. Health and fitness
___×____  8. Making a contribution to society
_____  9. Close personal friendships
_____ 10. A wide circle of acquaintances
_____ 11. Travel and vacation time
_____ 12. A successful career
___×____ 13. Pleasing and serving others
___×____ 14. Ethical work and lifestyle
_____ 15. A comfortable, attractive home
```

B. What motivates you at work? Mark your top five motivations.

  X   1. Career advancement

  X   2. Having a major impact

         3. Running a part of the business

         4. Earning a lot of money

         5. Achieving significant status

  X   6. Overcoming challenges

         7. Recognition of my achievements

         8. Being an authority in my field

         9. Learning and professional growth

         10. Autonomy and personal accountability

         11. Close relationships with colleagues ✓

         12. Having a high-profile role

         13. Maintaining organizational traditions

  X   14. Identifying with the organization

  X   15. Involvement in key decisions

C. How would you like to spend your time at work? Mark your top five preferences.

  X   1. Getting things right

         2. Developing others ✓

         3. Providing leadership

  X   4. Working hard to meet deadlines

         5. Influencing others to change

         6. Managing organizational change

         7. Being creative, innovative

         8. Facilitating a work team

         9. Personally serving customers ✓

         10. Negotiating with external stakeholders

_X_ 11. Developing more efficient methods
_X_ 12. Developing new products/services
_____ 13. Strategic planning
_X_ 14. Managing complex projects
_____ 15. Analyzing numbers accurately
_____ 16. Providing technical leadership

D. What would you like your experience at work to be? Mark the five items you desire most.

_____ 1. Having time for all I need to do
_____ 2. Delegating fully to others
_____ 3. Feeling okay to say no to extra work
_X_ 4. Not working too many hours
_____ 5. Getting regular feedback from my boss
_X_ 6. Receiving clear directions from management
_____ 7. Seeing individual employees perform well
_____ 8. Keeping open communication with colleagues
_____ 9. Avoiding company politics
_X_ 10. Getting my work done on time
_____ 11. Maintaining good relationships with my subordinates
_____ 12. Developing a good relationship with my boss
_X_ 13. Having good relationships with my peers
_____ 14. Seeing my team perform well
_____ 15. Being part of the overall organizational success
_X_ 16. Experiencing wide acceptance of my ideas
_____ 17. Having the respect/admiration of my colleagues

Now write out your top two choices for each section:

A. Personal Values
   1. *Pleasing & serving others*
   2. *Family*
B. Work Motivators
   1. *Career advancement*
   2. *Overcoming challenges*
C. How You'd Like to Spend Your Time at Work
   1. *Getting things right*
   2. *Working hard to meet deadlines*
D. How You'd Like Your Experience at Work to Be
   1. *Getting my work done on time*
   2. *Not working to many hours*

Now answer these two questions:

1. What conflict in values do you see arising from your answers?
If one of your key values is pleasing/serving others and your job involves supervising others to adhere to strict guidelines, you can see where you would feel conflict between these two areas. If it's important to you to get things right, yet your team is willing to sacrifice accuracy to speed, you have a value conflict. If you need regular feedback from your boss, but your boss barely knows your name, you're probably feeling the pinch of value conflict.

2. How do these value conflicts affect the way you do your job?
If you want to please people, but your job is to keep them in line, you may find yourself always trying to be nice so your employees will like you, rather than being consistent so they will respect you. If you're taking the

time to be accurate, you may be constantly harassed to hurry up and get the job done. If you keep asking an uncommunicative boss for feedback, your boss may see you as insecure and unable to handle your job independently. All of these conflicts will be reflected in your performance reviews and your opportunities for advancement.

Not everyone has the same values. You may feel compelled by one but repelled by another. Each of us is unique, a single expression of God's creation, and each of us carries a unique set of values. You can't force your values on others or on your organization. But you can change the way you react when value conflicts arise. If you recognize what turns your crank, and then see these values in the context of your job, you'll likely discover the reasons behind some of your dissatisfaction and frustration.

Does it seem hard to find God in all this?

The challenge is not to find God in the workplace but to let God find you. Instead of hiding behind feelings of frustration, doubt, fear, inadequacy, anger, impatience, apathy, or negativity, you can learn to cultivate the presence of God where you work.

WHAT MOTIVATES YOU?

Beyond your values is the deeper issue of motivation. What motivates you to get up in the morning, go to work, come home again, spend time with your family, and be involved in your community? Most people have at least one of the following motivators.

1. Personal Power

Personal power is how you feel about yourself at the innermost level. It involves your self-esteem, your confidence, and most importantly, your self-love. People with a high sense of personal power believe they can do anything set before them and face life's challenges with equanimity. If you're sure of your place in the universe, convinced that God cares for creation, then your sense of personal power is strong and deep. However, if you have trouble accepting the premise of a loving God, a God who will accept you as you are, One who loves you in all circumstances, at times you'll feel powerless and unimportant.

2. Achievement

Your most important motivator may be a sense of achievement. You set goals and then plan how to reach them. Sometimes your achievement is measured by winning, by making money, or by getting recognition. Your life is focused; you keep your eyes on the prize; you live according to your own life plan. Great athletes, top executives, and world leaders often have achievement as their key motivator. You may have difficulty with the idea of achievement being a motivator. Deep down, you feel uncomfortable climbing ladders or chasing dollars, feeling that your life should express more altruistic goals.

3. Intimacy

Humans need to feel close to each other. Robinson Crusoe, alone and abandoned on a desert island, longed for companionship. At some level, all of us long for intimacy: touching, feeling close, coupling, parenting, being a friend. This may be an overwhelming motivator for you—the need to belong, to love, to share is primary in everything you do. You may achieve this intimacy by becoming friends and confidants with some of your coworkers. Yet you may have found that expressing this intimacy—being open, honest, and caring—is seen as weakness in a leadership role. Although many organizations claim to want caring and compassionate managers and supervisors, in fact, these same caring and compassionate employees are often told to get tough and be more assertive.

4. Play and Creativity

Some people want to have fun. You may tell others, "You only live once," and "Life's too short to waste a moment." If a desire for play and creativity motivates you and you're in a job where this motivator is a primary function—theater, the arts, advertising—you probably feel happy and fulfilled. But if your job is based on routine and facts, prescribed by operating procedures and rules, you may feel stifled and frustrated. Your employees may see you as a time waster, frivolous, unable to be serious, and a disrupter of the work environment.

5. Search for Meaning

Do you feel as if you were born asking, "Why am I here? What is the meaning of life?" You may need to feel a connectedness with all things, to see wholeness in the world, to find inner peace and tranquility. Your life is spent in this quest, always searching for transcendence and bliss. If you could, you would spend your life in a monastery or out in the desert, deep in a cave or on a retreat, living in quiet contemplation. So what happens when you are thrust into a workday world? You're labeled as a dreamer or useless. You may find it hard to hold down a job, harder still to find meaning in it and see it as part of the divine plan for your life, and hardest of all to manage and motivate other people who don't have your profound need to connect with each other.

6. Compassion and Contribution

You may have been born to serve. Your primary motivator is giving, helping, feeding, improving, reforming, and volunteering. If you're able to work in organizations that offer social or environmental relief, then you feel as if you're doing something worthwhile, that you're actively making the world a better place. You may find yourself in a service occupation—

doctor, nurse, or social worker—a place where you can offer help and hope to those who need your care. It's easy to feel that you're in the right place when you're able to actively express love and care for others. However, if you find yourself in an organization where there's no opportunity to express compassion, no mandate to contribute to making the world a better place, you may feel that your workday world is a sham, that you're wasting your life, and that God has no place in your job. As a manager, you may struggle with your belief that a good leader serves others when your organization expects your role to be that of being served, whether through assigned work projects or team productivity.

DEALING WITH CONFLICT IN YOUR MOTIVATION

Too often, you may find that where you work doesn't feel right to you because your primary motivator for being alive is not expressed by your work. It would be wonderful if you could simply change jobs until you found the perfect fit, but in the real world, this is unlikely to happen. The old adage "bloom where you are planted" is a good one. If you can believe that God cares for you and has a plan for your life, then where you are right now is where you are meant to be. That's not to say that tomorrow the perfect job won't come along, but right now, here, in this moment, where you are is where you can connect to a higher power and use that power to achieve your goals in your workplace.

If you can't express your primary motivators within the context of your job, instead of feeling frustrated and unfulfilled, use the rest of your available time to act upon your primary motivators.

1. Personal Power

If you feel that you have no personal power on the job, try some of the following activities:

- Keep a journal, honestly expressing how you feel and what is happening in your world. Looking back over journal pages is an eye-opening experience and often pinpoints the places where you may invite the divine into your present.
- Spend time with people you admire and love. Listen to their wisdom. Open your heart to them.
- Give yourself some love. Begin to see yourself as a loved child of God. Treat yourself with care and respect.

2. Achievement

If one of your primary motivators is the desire for achievement, but you're stuck in what you consider to be a dead-end management position, here is an activity for you:

- Write out goals for yourself. Make these life goals instead of work goals. Your goals don't have to be big ones. In fact, it's best to start with some small goals until you begin to feel a sense of achievement in your life. For example, instead of saying, "I want to travel around the world," try a goal such as, "I want to go on a weekend trip to New York next July." Then plan to make this goal a reality. Get travel brochures, start a bank account, inquire about accommodations, check plane schedules.

3. Intimacy

If you long for intimacy in your daily life but don't find it where you work, there are ways to help you express this motivator:

- Befriend a neighbor you haven't spoken to.
- Get in touch with old friends.
- Go to lunch at least once a week with someone in your family or circle of friends.

4. Play and Creativity

If you desire more play and creativity in your life, yet your workplace is dull, bound by rules and traditions, and devoid of fun, try these activities:

- Sing in the car.
- Rent some old comedies at the video store.
- Volunteer to be with children and play with them.
- Sign up for a class: pottery making, acting, writing, painting.

5. Search for Meaning

If you feel that you have no opportunity for wholeness or peace in your workplace, search for meaning in your life in these ways:

- Go on a retreat.
- Take classes in meditation.
- Go for long walks in the woods, on the beach, in the park.
- Seek out older people and listen to their wisdom.
- Listen to fine music.

6. Compassion and Contribution

If you need to express compassion, to contribute, to make a difference in the world, but your role at work doesn't lend itself to this, try the following:

- Do a good deed anonymously.
- Instead of acquiring more stuff, give away some of your possessions.
- Volunteer at a soup kitchen, hospital, retirement home—anywhere that you can feel like you're contributing.
- Donate regularly to a service club, charity, or service organization.
- Join an advocacy group, whether it is Save the Whales, Bread for the World, or Mothers Against Drunk Driving.

You may never have a job where you can express your most important motivators, but that doesn't mean your place of work is a prison. If in the rest of life you are enjoying your primary motivators, then your time spent at work is not a burden you must bear but simply a part of your larger life. If you're not fretting about feeling inadequate, or not having enough recognition, or wishing for a closer relationships with your employees; if you're not wanting to have a little more fun and spontaneity on the job, or needing to feel that the job brings meaning to your life, or hating the sense of purposelessness in your workday, then you can get on with being a manager where you are. You'll be able to see God in the workplace, providing all you need to be a mindful manager.

This understanding that a higher power cares for you and what you do with your life, even within the confines of your nine-to-five job, is the first step in becoming a mindful manager.

2

DISCOVERING A PERSONAL VISION FOR YOUR WORKPLACE

Sometimes it's hard to let go of the past, especially when that past seems preferable to your present reality. Nowhere is this more evident than in the workplace. It was easier when your place in the corporate universe was firmly established. Organizational hierarchy ensured that you knew your job expectations, your reporting status, and the extent of your authority. This hierarchy was depicted as a pyramid, with the boss at the top and everyone else in descending order, down to the line workers at the broad base.

Your place on the pyramid determined your job in a straightforward way. You knew exactly how you fit into the organization, what job you were expected to do, for whom you did it, and to whom you could pass it on. You knew what positions were available to you and which route to take in order to reach those goals. The pyramid became your vision for your job. Best of all, you had the rules to keep you on track as you pursued this vision.

Today, many organizations have a hierarchy that blurs the lines of your vision. You may find yourself reporting to more than one person, having many job responsibilities, and/or working in several different areas. At the same time, you may have more responsibility, more personal power, and more input into how your job is done. Or you may have no responsibility, personal power, or input at all! Why? Because the rules have changed.

THE OLD RULES

The old rules were simple: be honest, work hard, obey the authorities, and you will experience security, success, happiness, and progress. Following the old rules, employees often stayed with the same company for all of their working lives. They were loyal to the organization, gave a full day's work, followed orders, and never questioned the direction of the company. In return they expected to be rewarded by regular pay raises, progressive promotions up the ladder of the hierarchy, and security in their jobs, with the result that everyone was happier at the end of the day. For many of these workers, the ultimate goal of their jobs was retirement, which meant a gold watch and a healthy pension.

Rules have always played an important part in the evolution of humankind. The book of Deuteronomy in the Hebrew scriptures is basically a rule book for living, somewhat like the standard operating procedures (SOPs) of most corporations. When Moses brought the Ten Commandments down from the mountain, he added another layer of obedience upon the Israelites.

When Jesus told his followers that the law was no longer needed, the average Pharisee felt that everything he had ever worked for and hoped to attain by strict adherence to the rules was now being offered to anyone, even to Gentiles! No wonder Jesus faced so much opposition.

In the workplace, there is the same dissention and chaos. The new rules only contribute to this feeling of impermanence and change.

THE NEW RULES

New Rule #1: You are not entitled.
No one owes you—not your parents, your teachers, your boss, your company, or even society. You cannot expect to be rewarded just because you are honest, work hard, and obey the authorities. This is a tough rule for many in the workforce. They feel entitled: that somebody somewhere owes them, just because they're on the earth.

New Rule #2: Change happens.
Change is not going away. What is today won't be the same tomorrow. In fact, the most successful companies embrace change, and those who say, "But that's not the way we've always done it," will find themselves left behind. Your company will change, your job will change, your boss will change, your duties will change, you will change. Before you've finished this paragraph, something somewhere will change.

New Rule #3: Your job is affected by global events.
The world is now so closely interwoven that a minor drought in some small South American nation can change the way your company does business. A flood in China, a hard winter in the Midwest, a political upheaval in a Baltic state, an assassination in Africa—all can affect your organization and your job. Global warming, dwindling oil stocks, rising fuel prices, post-9/11 security, the wars in Iraq and Afghanistan, free trade, fair trade, and even something as off-the-wall as a cloned sheep can have a profound ripple effect that spreads to the smallest company in the smallest town of this country.

New Rule #4: You need to recycle yourself in order to survive.
Remember when you were a child and grown-ups asked you, "What are you going to be when you grow up?" The answer was usually pretty

straightforward: a firefighter, a nurse, a doctor, a bus driver, an architect, a secretary, a teacher. Once you had a vision of what you wanted to be when you grew up, your task was to prepare yourself for that role. You went to school, took the right courses, passed your exams, and then you were declared to be a firefighter, a nurse, a doctor, a bus driver, an architect, a secretary, or a teacher. You then found a job in your chosen field and settled down to enjoy the fruits of your labor.

But that's probably not what happened. You may be one of those persons who got an honors degree in humanities, and now you manage a restaurant. Or your teaching certificate may be gathering dust in the closet as you work in a customer service center. You may have started out as a firefighter, but now you're working at computer repair. Or you might have trained to be an architect, but after the last round of layoffs, you're lucky to be a supervisor in the assembly plant. Unlike the lifetime career that was once the norm, you can expect to recycle yourself numerous times throughout your working life.

New Rule #5: Your lifestyle is your choice.
The class system is no longer a driving force in society, although remnants of it still remain. The vision for the United States and other industrialized countries is that career streams are open to everyone, regardless of social standing, wealth, gender, or race. While that may not always be true in practice, there is the understanding that the son of a janitor may aspire to be a doctor, the daughter of a wealthy socialite may choose to work in the barrios, and a woman can succeed in a political career. This new rule allows you greater freedom than ever before: the freedom to choose. It also allows you the freedom not to choose. That is, you may decide to live a simpler, less affluent lifestyle; opt for your personal life over your career success; or step off the career ladder to pursue other interests. Men can choose to stay

at home and take care of the children while their wives are the primary wage earners. Women can choose to delay childbearing while they focus on their careers. You face abundant choices that did not exist when jobs, workplaces, and careers were narrowly circumscribed by your social standing, gender, or race, not to mention your education or age.

New Rule #6: Follow your own vision for personal success.
Working hard and following corporate policies no longer guarantee you a secure job and workplace. Instead, it's up to you to find a vision for your job that will carry you forward through the good and bad times, sustaining you in work that may not be as fulfilling as you had hoped.

MINDFUL MANAGEMENT IN TURBULENT TIMES
You can't change the rules, but how you live your life can help you find the freedom that the new rules bring. By using six renewal strategies, you can reach a place where the new rules can't erode your desire to succeed as a manager in your workplace.

Strategy #1: Seek moments of solitude.
If you're rushing from meeting to meeting, dealing with personnel issues, working on new projects, ironing out old problems, handling irate customers, and keeping up with the paperwork that your position entails, there probably isn't much time in your busy day to listen to God's still, small voice. How do you find moments of solitude in your workday madness? How can you hear God speak to you amid the turbulence?

There are God-given quiet spaces in your hectic day—moments when you can pause, reflect on your current challenges, and give them to God, asking for wisdom and guidance as you continue your day. These stray minutes of unassigned time usually go unnoticed and unused.

You can find quiet spaces while you're on hold on the phone, standing in line at a restaurant, waiting for a meeting to begin, walking from one office to another, or grabbing a quick cup of coffee. These spare moments give you an opportunity to pray, saying something as simple as, "I have a meeting with Greg this afternoon. I'm dreading it, so I ask you to be with me as I talk to him about his work issues. Give me the words to say. Thank you." How long did that take? About ten seconds.

Ten seconds at a time, you can invite the divine to be part of your entire day. In those quiet spaces, you will often find that the solutions you seek come to your mind, the peace you need begins to still your worries, and an assurance of God's presence with you in your workplace gives you the strength to move through a difficult day.

Strategy #2: Have fun—every day.
Have you ever considered having fun in your workplace? Maybe not, since fun doesn't seem relevant to a business situation. The need is usually met somewhere else, such as on the golf course, during coffee break, in an exercise class, or at company parties. The need for fun is rarely met in day-to-day work relationships. Yet this need is important, not frivolous.

Think back to a time when your work group enjoyed themselves together. Perhaps you brought in donuts to a staff meeting, and suddenly the atmosphere changed. Your team members relaxed, made jokes, enjoyed the treat, and laughed together. Everyone seemed to be in a more mellow, more cooperative mood. All as a result of a box of donuts?

Not quite. The donuts were the beginning of a chain reaction. Because you set up the circumstances for a little enjoyment, your team members took the opportunity to enjoy themselves—just a little. There was laughter.

When humans laugh, two things happen: (1) They learn easier, and (2) They heal faster.

An apocryphal story is told of a group of third-grade schoolchildren. Half the class was taught a history subject by an excellent teacher who used classic teaching methods. The other half was taught the same subject by a teacher dressed as a clown who made the children laugh. At the end of the teaching period, both groups were tested on the information taught to them. The children in the group who laughed as they learned scored significantly higher than the group taught in the traditional manner. The story may or may not be true. However, in a study pointing to humor's benefits, psychologist Randy Garner found that students were more likely to recall a statistics lecture when it was interspersed with jokes about relevant topics.[1]

Laughing releases your creativity and turns on the learning mechanisms in your brain. You make better decisions, take more risks, and cooperate more with others when you have fun. Something else happens when you laugh. Laughter triggers the release of endorphins, the natural painkillers of your body, into the bloodstream. Have you ever noticed that you forget your aches and pains when you're enjoying yourself?[2]

Your team will feel better and function more efficiently when it has the opportunity for fun and creativity. So how can you bring fun and creativity into your workplace? Try providing yourself (and your staff) with some toys—things like modeling clay, marbles, jacks, building blocks. Leave one or two lying on your desk or on the conference room table, and see what happens. People will play with them, and so will you. Barriers come down. Communication opens up. Laughter begins. Give yourself permission to play like a child at least once every working day.

Strategy #3: Create an inner circle.

Can you remember having a boss or a teacher who played favorites? Unless you were the favorite, it probably isn't a good memory. It's tough not to enjoy working with some people more than others. Some people are just naturally easier to get along with, more cooperative, more friendly, more willing to give that extra 10 percent when the chips are down. There are people with whom you enjoy an instant rapport and understanding.

Key relationships that form an inner circle are different from friendships. Key relationships are business-oriented—based on the skills, abilities, influence, and knowledge of the various people around you. If you are fortunate enough to have a mentor, then that person would be a key relationship for you in your workplace. If you have a subordinate to whom you can delegate some of your responsibilities when you aren't there, that is another key relationship to add to your inner circle.

Key relationships form your support network. This network is made up of relationships you've established, both inside and outside the company, relationships based on mutual goodwill, trust, and a willingness to help.

Management is not an individual sport—it is a process of utilizing people from the informal and formal organization to accomplish goals. How do you learn how to use the informal organization and establish a reciprocal network for you and your department?

1. Move around the organization. Look for groups and people who can provide your department with needed resources.
2. Develop a support network and use it. Ask for supportive action where it will do the most good and look for an opportunity to return a favor.

Strategy #4: Leave your home life at home.
Most books on management principles will tell you to leave your home life at home, and your work life at work. It always looks good on paper, but in practice, it's difficult to forget about that squabble with your

teenager, that call from the doctor's office about your partner's test results, the pile of bills sitting on the dining room table, or the upcoming meeting with your son's teachers.

You may think that these home issues don't affect how well you carry out your job responsibilities, but in fact, they do. If your mind is filled with thoughts of home-related worries, it's hard to focus on the task before you. Your team will feel your distraction, recognize your mood swings, and resent your lack of attention to their needs and the job at hand.

No one has a perfect home life. It is the nature of relationships to go through cycles of intensity and challenge. However, you can take steps to lessen personal distractions at work.

1. If something negative is going on in your life, focus on a positive aspect of your home life instead.
2. Carry some personal physical reminder with you of what is positive in your life. For example, a small seashell from your beach trip will bring back the positive feelings you had there.
3. Consciously give that negative personal challenge to your higher power as you walk into your office in the morning by saying something like, "God, I don't want to think about those test results while I'm working. I'm giving them to you. Thank you." Throughout the day, as you feel your mind drifting back to the distraction, repeat the prayer.

Strategy #5: Get your personal financial ducks lined up.
Develop a financial plan that includes a budget for your expenses, charities, and savings. If necessary, visit a financial planner to help you get your finances in order. You may find that you're not as rich as you'd like to be, or as free from debt as you should be, or as able to spend money as you want to be. But at least you'll know where you are. By staying within your

budget, you have a clear idea of the options available to you, and you take the money worries off your mind.

Why is this necessary? Money worries are the number-one reason many people stay in jobs they hate. How many times have you heard someone say, or perhaps have said yourself, "I hate the job, but I need the money"?

Doing a job, any job, that you hate is soul destroying. And, doing a job that involves management of others and hating every moment will never be a mindful way of working. When you see that the money you earn in your job can meet your requirements, then you can put your energy and your passion into making that job part of a vision for your wider life. Having a financial plan is a matter of being a wise steward of what God has given you today.

Strategy #6: Have a deep sense of purpose.
The story is told of a pedestrian passing by a building site where several laborers were working. "What are you doing?" he asked them.

"I'm digging a hole," was the terse reply from one.

"What does it look like? I'm mixing cement," said the second.

"I'm laying bricks," said the third, slapping another brick down.

But the fourth worker, a light of interest and enthusiasm in his eyes, declared, "I'm building a cathedral."

The work you do may not always be exciting. Not all managers have big paychecks, the corner office, accolades from the boss, or admiration from their employees. Like the workers at the construction site, your job may seem like just digging holes and mixing cement.

However, if you know that your job is part of your vision, then you can see it as the fourth worker did. Any work is exciting and fulfilling when you know it is part of a larger plan for your life.

Finding a Personal Vision

Do you have a personal vision for your life? Do you know what you want to do and what you need to do in order to get there? Most people don't. They simply go along, day by day, letting things happen or not happen, with no thought about how the events of their days fit into the vision of their lives.

Before you can begin to have a vision for your job—that pesky portion of your life that takes up so much of your gray matter and your energy—you should have a broad vision of who God created you to be.

You can spend hours, days, even years, formulating a personal vision, but if you'd like to take a shortcut, try this simple exercise.

1. List some roles you'd like to play in order to live your life in a mindful way. Write down every role you can think of. Don't allow yourself to be too critical of your choices. Don't worry about whether you have the skills, experience, education, resources, or the time to play these roles. Just jot them down as they occur to you. Think of roles like friend, volunteer, teacher, helper, musician.

   Leader, husband, planner, father, Creator

   _____

   _____

2. List the positive attributes or inherent characteristics that your dearest friends and family say you possess. All of us have some qualities that others have admired or pointed out. It may be something like your ability to see the positive side of any situation, your honesty, your sense of fun, your faithfulness, or your integrity.

Patience, kindness

3. List characteristics you'd like to see in the world around you. Think of all those things you've always wished would happen. Perhaps you'd like to see the end of world hunger, equality for all peoples and races, church harmony, peace, protection of children, or freedom for oppressed peoples.

equality for di gnity, (human)

4. Choose two of your God-given skills or abilities. This is not the time to be modest. Be honest. Everyone has something that he or she does well, whether it is being able to repair an engine, whip up a great meal in minutes, listen to others, sing, or make friends easily.

Fill the blanks in the following statement, using your own answers from the four questions.

I am committed to being a _____ (answer from #1) and a _____ (answer from #1) by expressing my _____ (answer from #2) and _____ (answer from #2). **While navigating through life's challenges, I will seek to promote** _____ (answer from #3) **and** _____ (answer from #3). **I invest my gifts of** _____ (answer from #4) **and** _____ (answer from #4) **in my community.**

There you have it: a short, succinct, and action-oriented spiritual vision for your life.

You can have the same kind of vision for your job as a manager. First, answer the following questions:

1. To be a good manager, what are some roles you need to play?

   leader, planner, visionary, problem solver

   _____

   _____

2. What positive attributes have your performance reviews indicated you possess?

   _____

   _____

_____

3. What characteristics would you like to see in your department?

Consistency _____

_____

_____

4. What are your God-given skills or abilities that make you a good manager?

_____

_____

_____

Complete the following statement, using your answers above.

I am committed to being a _____ (answer from #1) **and a** _____ (answer from #1), **by expressing my** _____ (answer from #2) **and** _____ (answer from #2). **While navigating through the challenges of my workplace, I will seek to promote** _____ (answer from #3) **and** _____ (answer from #3). **I**

invest my gifts of _____ (answer

from #4) and _____ (answer

from #4) in my employees and in my department.

Write out your workplace managerial vision and place it where you can see it daily. Memorize it. Repeat it to yourself as you step off the elevator, go into that difficult staff meeting, begin the performance reviews with your staff, or deal with conflict in the department. Make it your mantra in all situations, and continually strive toward the vision you have set for yourself.

Your vision is now a concrete image of what God can do through you in your daily life. Be mindful of it in every situation you face in the workplace.

→ I need to work on not being seen as harsh, judgemental, or negative.

3

RESTRUCTURING YOUR INTERNAL POWER BASE

IAMNOWHERE.

What did you just read? *I am nowhere?* Look again. *I am now here.* Same letters. Same place. You may feel nowhere in your job. It may seem like you are just treading water, marking time, waiting for a better opportunity. You may feel stuck, trapped, out of options, out of control, and powerless to change the course of your life.

Or perhaps you feel you are at a good place in your career. You may feel in control of what is happening on the job, in the place you have chosen to be, doing the work you love to do.

The paradox is that whether you see your situation as a helpless nowhere or as an exciting present, both are "now here." This place, this situation, this attitude is what God has to work with. It's the starting point for all that is to come after this moment. Seeing where you are as the "now here" of God's plan is the beginning of understanding your internal power and how it relates to the way you do your job.

WHERE IS HERE?

Before you begin to assess your internal power base, take a few minutes to determine what "now here" is for you. A number of aspects to our lives contribute to our feeling of well-being—who we are, what we are, what we desire, what we have. Rate the following aspects of your life on a scale of 1 to 10, with 10 being very unsatisfactory and 1 being very satisfactory.

1. My Job: 1 2 3 (4) 5 6 7 8 9 10

Consider your current work position. Is it all you'd hoped it would be? Is it part of your career path? Is it as satisfying as it could be? Are you happy with your position in the company?

2. My Family: 1 2 3 4 5 6 7 8 9 10

What kind of home life do you have? Is it satisfying? Do you look forward to going home at the end of your workday? Do you get love and support from your family?

3. My Community: 1 2 3 4 5 6 7 8 9 10

How well do you like where you live? Do you have friends in the community? Are you involved in community groups or projects? Do you feel safe and secure in your community?

4. My Health: 1 2 3 4 5 6 7 8 9 10

How is your health in general? Do you have chronic disease or health challenges? Do you worry about your health? Are there family health issues that cause you concern?

5. My Strengths: 1 2 3 4 5 6 7 8 9 10

How aware are you of your strengths? Do you have strengths that support you in tough times? Do you have strengths that enhance your job?

6. My Challenges: 1   2   3   4   5   6   7   8   9   10
How challenging is your life? Do you feel capable of meeting most of your challenges—in other words, do they make your life exciting and fulfilling? Or are you feeling overwhelmed by the challenges in your life?

7. My Goals: 1   2   3   4   5   6   7   8   9   10
Are you happy with where you are going? Have you set realistic goals for your life? Do you feel that you've accomplished some of them?

Now take a look at your ratings for these aspects of your life. With 1–5 being satisfactory ratings and 6–10 being unsatisfactory, which side has the most answers? Generally speaking, this will determine whether your "now here" is a place that causes you to feel unhappy or happy. The aspects with the highest numbers are those areas where you feel the greatest challenges and are the cause of unhappiness or stress in your life. The aspects with the lowest numbers are those areas that bring you the greatest happiness and keep you going when things get tough. Taken together, these aspects of your life will probably determine whether you're basically a positive or a negative person.

There is more to the "now here" of your life than just the aspects on your satisfactory/unsatisfactory scale. The elements of your self-esteem also play a role in how you perceive your position in life.

The ideas that you hold about yourself and the world around you make up your self-esteem. Usually these ideas are unconscious and unexamined, but almost every action you take is influenced by them. They're often the root cause of why you act the way you do.

Your self-esteem comes from your past, especially from adults you knew in childhood. Most of your self-esteem beliefs were formed before you were six years old. If adults told you that you were bright, lovable, and creative, you enjoyed a positive belief in your abilities. On the other hand, if adults said you were stupid, lazy, or useless, their negative statements created a belief in your own unworthiness. These are very simplistic, black-and-white statements of self-esteem. Self-esteem is actually a lot more complicated. It's based on conflicting statements from the adults around you, your own experiences when dealing with your self-esteem issues, and your expectations of yourself and your behavior. If your self-esteem explains why you behave in certain ways, then it also plays a key role in your behavior as a manager.

Managers with a high sense of self-esteem operate from a positive framework of belief that gives them a personal power base upon which to rest their management decisions.

FIVE KEY ELEMENTS OF YOUR PERSONAL POWER BASE

1. Self-Responsibility

One of the key words in the job description of a manager is *responsibility*. As a manager, you're expected to take responsibility for your personal workload, your department's workload, and your ability to get things accomplished. Most managers accept this responsibility and enjoy a feeling of satisfaction when their work goals are met by themselves and their employees. Some, however, may have trouble with the fact that if something does go wrong, the responsibility is on their shoulders. For these managers, when something doesn't work out the way they expected it to, they might say, "Why does this always happen to me?" Such a response reflects a belief that they have no power over their lives. Some may feel victimized by a life circumstance, attempting to put the blame on something or someone else. They may feel helpless and out of control. They may feel their higher power is punishing them.

This fear of self-responsibility is a common response from some people when they are appointed as a manager. In addition to excitement at the prospect of the new job and responsibilities, there may also be the thought, *Why me? I can't do this. I don't know how.*

2. Self-Worth

Someone once defined self-worth as loving yourself, warts and all. To not only accept yourself but also love yourself as an imperfect, changing, growing, worthwhile person is the essence of self-worth. How do you feel about yourself? Do you think you are a lovable person? Do you find it easy to accept praise and compliments from other people? Do you feel you deserve success in your life? Do you know that God loves you?

If your feelings of self-worth are low, you may experience doubts about your ability to handle the job of manager. You may even believe that you don't deserve this responsibility because you're not "good enough." Such doubts will transfer to your interactions with your staff.

3. Outlook on Life

Do you see life as a problem to be overcome or as an opportunity to be experienced? Your mental outlook on all the events of your life will influence its outcome. In many ways, you are a self-fulfilling prophecy: you get what you expect. Do you expect the abundant life God promises us? Or do you expect to be continually tested with difficulties and troubles?

A positive outlook doesn't mean being a Pollyanna who thinks that everything is wonderful, regardless of the circumstances. Nor does it mean burying your head in the sand like an ostrich. A positive outlook means realistically assessing what you can achieve in any situation. It requires courage and strength of mind to face whatever life brings you and to find the good, the positive, and the opportunities that lie there.

People naturally respond to someone who expects the best from them and the situation.

4. Personal Security

When you feel secure about your place in the universe and sense that you are part of a larger plan for your life, you're willing to take some risks. You're able to give up control when needed and trust others to support you. If you feel that where you are right now aligns with God's plans for you, then you'll feel secure in your position. But if you feel that you're in a tenuous position, with only your own wits and cunning to protect you, you're probably feeling alone and afraid.

Managers with a low sense of personal security tend to be dictatorial. They seldom see themselves as part of the team. In fact, they usually feel isolated and set apart from their employees.

5. Attitude toward Change

Many people have the illusion that stability is the law of nature. In fact, the reverse is true. Nature is continuously in a state of change—growing, evolving, expanding, breaking down, dying, and renewing. All of humankind is in a similar state of change.

Do you get upset when something unexpected occurs? Are you anxious when circumstances change? Do you resist change and feel secure only when things remain the same? Do you insist that your employees do things the same way they've always been done? An attitude that sees all change as threatening can make you rigid and inflexible.

These core elements of self-esteem are worth examining, since they can help you discover why you may be experiencing difficulty in your role as a manager. Your self-esteem issues directly affect how well you function as a leader.

When You Feel Inadequate

Self-esteem plays a role in every aspect of our lives. We all have moments when we feel powerless, uncomfortable, nervous, worried, out of our depth, angry, upset, intimidated, inferior, shy, or stupid. That's part of the human psyche. Some hide their feelings a little better than others, but the bottom line is that all people, regardless of their position in life or their personal power, have times when they feel inadequate.

How you deal with feeling inadequate is a key to how you handle the people you supervise. The following quiz will give you some insights into the kinds of behaviors you use in these moments when your self-esteem is challenged.

What Do You Value on the Job?

Rank each item below from 1 to 10, with 1 being most important to you and 10 being least important.

1. Career success		1	2	3	4	5	6	7	8	9	10
2. Challenging work		1	2	3	4	5	6	7	8	9	10
3. Getting along with peers		1	2	3	4	5	6	7	8	9	10
4. Achievement of company goals		1	2	3	4	5	6	7	8	9	10
5. Family time		1	2	3	4	5	6	7	8	9	10
6. Personal income		1	2	3	4	5	6	7	8	9	10
7. Respect of peers		1	2	3	4	5	6	7	8	9	10
8. Contribution to society		1	2	3	4	5	6	7	8	9	10
9. Sense of belonging		1	2	3	4	5	6	7	8	9	10
10. Meeting personal goals		1	2	3	4	5	6	7	8	9	10

Items 1, 2, 4, 6, 10:

If you put a value between 1 and 5 on at least three of these items, you may be ambitious and hardworking and enjoy a greater degree of authority. When your self-esteem is challenged, you probably use authoritarian methods to deal with your staff—giving orders, refusing to discuss, arbitrarily making decisions. You compensate for your fear of not having all the information needed to make the right decision by constantly seeking more information, asking more questions, and avoiding decisions. You can get caught up in the process of making decisions and forget the importance of reaching a conclusion. You're likely to constantly ask your staff to give you reports, projections, futuristic scenarios, and alternative answers. Your department grinds to a halt because no decisions are ever made. Your staff sees you as someone who makes work difficult with your constant demands for information. They avoid doing anything because they know it won't make any difference but instead will become part of the backlog of paper you already have on your desk.

If you put a value between 6 and 10 on at least three of these items, you may not be as ambitious as others. You may have trouble believing that you can manage others, and you may not be comfortable with your authority and responsibility. When you're feeling inadequate, you may abdicate your position, allowing others to make decisions and determine their own workloads.

Items 3, 5, 7, 8, 9:
If you put a value between 1 and 5 on at least three of these items, you probably are a people person with strong management/supervisory skills. When your self-esteem is challenged, you may become a people pleaser who looks for input from all of your staff before making a decision because you fear displeasing them. You may become afraid of others and be easily swayed. In an effort to deal with your feeling of inadequacy in the situation, you capitulate to your staff, allowing them to take advan-

tage of you. You try to be too nice, and as a result, alienate those who feel that you haven't favored them as much as others. You want everyone to agree with a decision before it is implemented and may avoid making decisions that might prove to be unpopular. Your staff will see you as weak, vacillating, and unable to lead from a position of authority or strength. They will take advantage of you at every opportunity, and you'll feel that you've lost control of your department.

If you put a value between 6 and 10 on at least three of these items, you may be an authoritarian manager who thinks it's more important to get the work done than to make people happy. When you're challenged, you probably withdraw from the group and issue deadlines, ultimatums, and work orders. As you try to compensate for your feelings of inadequacy, you may believe that your people have an inherent dislike of work and will try to avoid it whenever possible. You think they'll only achieve goals and accomplishments if pushed or bullied by you. You believe that they don't want responsibility, and it's up to you to be the tough boss, enforcing the rules and applying discipline if necessary. Your staff may see you as cold, unfeeling, someone who watches their every move and is quick to judge and punish.

RESTRUCTURING YOUR POWER BASE

To avoid these extremes of behavior as a manager, develop a power base to fall back upon in those times when you're feeling inadequate. Here are key components of that power base.

Positional vs. Personal Power

As a manager, you can act from a position of power. You usually have authority to make sure that your employees do the job they are being paid to perform. Like it or not, this positional power sets you apart from your employees, and the habits that are left over from the old hierarchical form of organizations means that employees will often leave the decision making and responsibility to you. They may give lip service with no enthusiasm or energy.

What kind of power should you demonstrate? Personal power! Personal power is not conferred on you by the higher authorities in your organization but comes from within. It is based on your beliefs in your own worth—your self-esteem—and allows you to use your skills, abilities, and strengths to contribute to the success of your team. It is a long way from the positional power role of telling people what to do.

The mindful manager understands that personal power comes from a higher power and transcends the earthly beliefs that can affect self-esteem. Despite what you may have been told in your early formative years, who and what you are today is based on how God views you, not on how other humans view you. God is beyond time and can obliterate the negative messages you may have received from people in your life. Your self-esteem now can be based solely on God, and your personal power becomes a God-centered energy. Those same key elements that contributed to your self-esteem can now become the building blocks for a personal power that comes not from your inner beliefs and history but from a loving God.

God-Responsibility vs. Self-Responsibility

It is always easier to blame something or somebody for how you feel or act. "Well, no wonder I'm stressed out. I have huge time demands and very difficult people to deal with." Avoiding responsibility for your actions and your feelings is often a sign of low self-esteem, but for the mindful manager, it's a sign that you're no longer in touch with God in that particular aspect of your job.

That's not to say that you no longer have any responsibility in the matter at all. We are creatures who have been given self-determination, but to be a mindful manager is to bring God into your workplace, listening for divine promptings, and gaining personal power from a higher power than yours.

Your Worth as a Loved Child of God

If you base your self-worth on how others treat you, then you may become a person whose life is spent trying to please others. As a manager, you may find it particularly challenging to discipline your employees, offer negative feedback when necessary, or deal with conflicts in the workplace because you're afraid of what others might say about you or feel toward you.

You can't force people to like you, but you can earn their respect by being straightforward, fair, and honest with them. You can be a manager who deals boldly and fairly with the more difficult aspects of the job. If you believe that you are a loved child of God, your self-worth then becomes God-centered rather than people-centered.

One of the easiest ways to strengthen your self-worth is to use what most likely took away your self-worth in the first place—words. Instead of telling yourself, "I'm no good at disciplining my staff," or "He's going to hate me if I do this," try giving yourself some positive reinforcement. Tell yourself, "God is with me. In God's eyes, I am a whole person."

Words are more powerful than you can imagine. They work on your subconscious mind until what you say becomes a deep-rooted truth. The manager who can believe that she is a loved child of God will have fewer troubles with feelings of self-worth when it comes time to deal with staff issues.

A God-Powered Outlook on Life

It is impossible to be upbeat and optimistic every moment of every day. You may have down days when the glass looks half empty. You may get depressed, down in the mouth, upset, and worried. As a human being, you have emotions, and it is unrealistic to expect to be in a positive frame of mind all the time.

You haven't lost sight of your goal to be a mindful manager if you're having a down day. But if you allow your negative moment to overwhelm your entire consciousness and then transmit that negativity to the people around you, you've moved away from connecting with the divine, the spiritual. Negativity is contagious. It doesn't take much to bring down the morale of the whole group until everyone is indulging in an "ain't it awful" session.

Being mindful is remembering that God is with you in every aspect of your day. When you feel negative and unhappy, that's the time to remind yourself that a higher power is still present. You may not feel instantly positive and energized, but you will feel uplifted and sustained. That sense of being above the circumstances will carry over to your staff, and they'll respond to your determination to seek the positive in the situation.

Trust in God's Protection and Caring

If you feel that you are all alone in life, that people will take advantage of you if you let them, that you have to look out for yourself because no one else will, and that you need to be in control all the time, you may believe that in our world no one is safe. This is not the world we are promised. In a spiritually centered life, a trust in God's protection and caring allows you to step out of your comfort zone, move beyond the daily ruts of safety, and take risks that might seem foolish to others.

Trusting in God means that you can let go and move through life freely and boldly, daring to be open with your employees, trusting them to support you and the work you do. When you understand that your security comes from God, you feel secure in your place in the universe. You can give up control when needed and trust others to support you.

The Unchanging God

For some reason, change is seen as a negative force in the world. Someone once said that the only person who likes change is a baby with a wet diaper! You change daily and so does your world.

Do you find that thought frightening? Do you fight change, clinging to the way it always was, longing for the good old days, dreaming of returning to a kinder, less frenetic time? It can't be done. Change is here to stay.

Yet in the midst of change, there is one immutable law: God does not change. God's power, love, and presence are constant, unchanging, and timeless. This assurance is all you need to combat the feeling that change is overwhelming you and leaving you battered and bruised in its wake.

Hold on to that surety in all that you do. Remind yourself of the unchanging love of God in the face of a world of change and upheaval. Thank God that you and your place in the universe are secure.

Remember the five steps to claiming your God-centered power base:

1. Choose to live a God-centered life.
2. Believe that you are a loved child of God.
3. Expect God to uplift and sustain you in all circumstances.
4. Trust that your security comes from God.
5. Believe that God is unchanging.

With these five steps, you have the foundation of a God-centered power base that allows you to move away from old, self-destructive behaviors. Your "now here" experience is tempered with the new sense of self-esteem that comes from knowing that your higher power is an integral part of the work you do.

PART TWO

COPING WITH THE WORLD AROUND YOU

STRESS, TIME, AND CHANGE are three key factors that can mean the difference between a wonderful day on the job or a nightmare day in the salt mines!

When your day is filled with stressors—late buses, bad-tempered bank clerks, angry employees, crunching deadlines, missed meetings, lost memos, new projects, old problems, and everything in between—it is hard to remember that God is concerned with what is happening in your life.

When time is running out—on your morning commute, your parking meter, your monthly report, your meeting agenda, your to-do list, and your clock—it is hard to remember that time is a limitless resource from God.

When change is ongoing in your workplace and each day brings new challenges—from a change in your office configuration, to a change in your responsibilities, to a change in procedures, to a change in computer programs—it is comforting to remember that God is unchanging.

4

FINDING GOD IN A
STRESSFUL WORKPLACE

Are there days when you feel your stress level mounting? One thing piles on top of another until you think you can't take another minute without howling in sheer frustration. Your head aches, your muscles ache; in fact, your whole body aches, and all you want to do is go home, bury your head under the covers, and come out some time next month.

But you don't. You soldier on. You take a deep breath, say a prayer, ignore your headache and the cramp in your stomach, paste on a smile, and somehow make it through the day.

Does it seem that stress at work is getting worse? Today's workforce faces many more stressful issues than those of the past: the tyranny of now, the ever-changing work environment, the insecurity of the organization, the reality of information overload—all contribute to stress on the job.

Add to that the manager's role in the workplace, and it is no wonder you are feeling stressed. Managers don't just manage anymore. Now you're expected to nurture, guide, lead, mentor, empower, and counsel your employees. You're supposed to be empathetic, sympathetic, a great communicator, and an everyday cheerleader. In addition, you're expected to elicit enthusiasm and loyalty from the people who report to you, despite the stressors that exist in your workplace.

There's a perception that those who have faith in God shouldn't experience negative stress. Sounds good in theory, but in practice, it is easy to become overwhelmed by the people, places, events, situations, and things around you, in spite of your spiritual beliefs. There is a paradox in knowing that you can trust God to uphold you in any situation, but when you're in the midst of the stressful moment, you may not remember that God is there with you.

Many of the stressors you face every day are subtle and insidious. Only when you realize that you're stressed out and overwhelmed do you remember God's presence. By this time, you and those around you are paying the physical, mental, and spiritual price for your stress.

What's causing you stress in your workplace? Here's a simple self-test to help you pinpoint some of the sources of stress that may be troubling you.

TEN RISK FACTORS FOR STRESS

1. Negative Perception Habits
When you think of your job, do you always look on the gloomy side? Do you seem to get up on the wrong side of the bed every morning? Do you expect things to go wrong?

Having a negative perception habit means that it's difficult for you to see the positive aspects of your job. You probably didn't start out that way. Like most people, you enjoyed your job in the beginning. However, as your on-the-job stress mounted, it became tougher to remain positive. If your workplace is also rife with negativity, it's almost impossible to keep from being infected with the negativity bug.

Rate your negative perception habit on a scale of 1 to 5, with 1 being *not at all* and 5 being *very much so.* 1 2 3 4 5

2. Management Pressures

Many managers aren't prepared for the pressures that management brings. From the perspective of other employees, managers seem to have it made. You make decisions, have meaningful work, interact with others in the organization, and enjoy the perks and privileges of your position.

You do have privileges others don't, but you've probably discovered that a lot of baggage comes with being a manager. This baggage presents itself in the form of pressures that contribute to your daily stress. These pressures come in many guises, from deadline pressures to staffing issues, from lack of resources to lack of authority, from difficult employees to disciplinary problems.

Rate the management pressures you experience on a scale of 1 to 5, with 1 being *not at all* and 5 being *very much so.* 1 2 3 4 5

3. Environmental Issues

Some stressors in the workplace are beyond your control. They probably affect the others in your organization as well and can contribute to a general sense of depression and despair.

Economic environmental issues resulting from a failing economy begin to put pressure on your organization to survive. Rising taxes and inflation can affect the products of your organization and change the customer base and market share, which in turn affect your sense of security and well-being in the company.

Geographic environmental issues can be based purely on where you work. Perhaps your building or plant is in poor physical condition, with old offices and obsolete equipment. If your workplace is located in a run-down neighborhood, this will contribute to your stress levels.

Rate how environmental issues in your workplace affect you on a scale of 1 to 5, with 1 being *not at all* **and 5 being** *very much so.* 1   2   3   4   5

4. Work Problems

Work problems outside of your specific management duties can create stress for you. For example, if your job is boring, you'll find that the boredom you experience spills over into your sense of enjoyment and well-being.

Conflict with people on the job is a large factor in creating stress. Perhaps your management group is causing you trouble. If you are feeling unappreciated, that you don't fit in with the group, or that the group isn't doing their fair share of the workload, you'll experience stress when you deal with them.

Your employees or work group can be a source of stress. It may be the attitude of the whole team or just one person who is making it difficult for you to enjoy the work you do.

Perhaps some of your stress comes from feeling too much pressure to perform. If standards are impossible to meet, if too much is expected of you, or if you have a boss who is hard to please, work becomes a stress-ful place for you.

Rate how work problems affect you on a scale of 1 to 5, with 1 being *not at all* **and 5 being** *very much so.* 1   2   3   4   5

5. Helper Mentality

Do you find yourself trying to respond to everyone else's needs all the time? Do you believe it's your job to fix things and make things right? Do you spend a lot of time trying to sort out other people's problems? Some people seem to have a built-in need to shoulder the burdens and problems of everyone around them.

You may feel pressured to smooth things over and keep everyone happy in your group. If you're spending a large proportion of your time putting out fires rather than managing—if you're beginning to feel put upon, used, or taken for granted—then you're probably dealing with the stress resulting from a helper mentality.

Rate how having a helper mentality affects you from 1 to 5, with 1 being *not at all* **and 5 being** *very much so.* 1   2   3   4   5

6. Responsibility without Resources, Authority, or Gratitude

Do you have a job to do without permission to do it your way? Do you have a job to do without the resources to do it well? Do you have a job to do without any appreciation or thanks?

In a study conducted to find out which jobs caused the greatest stress, occupations such as airline flight controllers, emergency room doctors, and firefighters scored less stress than teachers, office workers, and managers. Why? Because those who worked in what were perceived as occupations with a great deal of stress also had the resources and authority to do their jobs, and they were usually thanked for doing their jobs. However, teachers, office workers, and managers who were perceived to have low stress actually experienced high levels of stress because they didn't have the resources or authority to do their jobs well. In addition, they seldom received gratitude or thanks for doing the job well.

Rate how a lack of resources, authority, and gratitude affects you on a scale of 1 to 5, with 1 being *not at all* **and 5 being** *very much so.* 1   2   3   4   5

7. Negative Coping Patterns

Are you using faulty stress safety valves? Do you find yourself getting angry, annoyed, even abusive on the job? Or do you withdraw, lapse into passivity, and simply opt out? Do you confront or ignore? Shout or use silence? Blame or overexcuse? Do you suffer from guilt as a result of these actions and then overcompensate by trying to be nice and make up for your negative feelings and behaviors?

When stress strikes, how you cope with it reveals how much power that particular stressor has over your life. Responding negatively often compounds the stress. If you allow the stressor to cause you to lose your temper, you'll suffer more than if you deal with the stressor in a more positive way. Do you respond to the stress in your workplace in any of these negative ways—denial, overindulgence, illness, revenge, tantrums, withdrawal, worrying, passivity, stubbornness, faultfinding, or anger?

Rate how negative coping patterns affect you on a scale from 1 to 5, with 1 being *not at all* and 5 being *very much so*. 1 2 3 4 5

8. Experiencing Lack of Purpose

A job should give you a sense of accomplishment and satisfaction. If you work in an environment where you feel you have no purpose or goals, you'll experience stress. If your workplace has values that conflict with yours—if they are focused on financial gain while you are focused on customer satisfaction—your stress levels will rise. If your job doesn't address what is really important to you, your job becomes a source of stress.

Rate your experience of purposelessness on a scale of 1 to 5, with 1 being *not at all* and 5 being *very much so*. 1 2 3 4 5

9. Health Worries

Are you suffering from a personal illness that affects the way you perform your management duties? Or is a close family member experiencing health challenges?

When you are focused on your health or on the health of someone you love, it is hard to pay attention to the day-to-day issues of your workplace. Even when you try to pray about your current problem, it's not uncommon to find that you are centered on the crisis and its outcome, rather than on God. Faced with the reality of the infirmity of our earthly bodies, the demands of the job seem less important, and it may be almost impossible for you to give the job more than lip service.

Rate your health worries on a scale of 1 to 5, with 1 being *not at all* and 5 being *very much so*. 1 2 3 4 5

10. Professional Life Changes

Are you making less money than you once did? Has your job recently changed substantially? Have you lost a valued employee? Do you have a new boss? Have major changes taken place in the organization?

Change may be an ever-present reality in today's workplace, but that doesn't make it any less stressful. Even when the change is positive, it can affect your stress levels. Some health-care professionals use a life-change analysis to determine the level of stress in their patients. The analysis includes events such as a desired promotion at work, a raise in salary, or the successful completion of a challenging task, as well as negative events such as the loss of a job, change to a difficult boss, and decrease in salary. The more events that happen to the patient in a set period of time, usually one year, the more likely the patient suffers from severe stress and the resulting physical consequences.

Score the professional life changes you experience on a scale of 1 to 5, with 1 being *not at all* and 5 being *very much so*. 1 2 3 4 5

Add up your score from all ten areas. _____

If you scored between 10 and 20: Congratulations! It isn't your job that is causing your stress.

If you scored between 20 and 40: You're probably finding that a good deal of your stress is coming from your job.

If you scored between 40 and 50: Hang on tight! Your job is probably your major stressor right now.

STRESS IS HOW YOU LOOK AT IT

Before you can address the stressors that you have on your job, it's important to understand how stress works.

Stress is the result of a reaction. It's measured in feelings and by the actions that result from these feelings. For example, your employee comes in late for the third time in a week. You feel annoyed and frustrated, perhaps even angry. When you speak sharply to the employee, you're feeling stressed.

When you react to a person, place, event, situation, or thing, it becomes a stressor. There has to be a catalyst for the stress to begin. Something triggers your reaction, which in turn triggers your feelings and actions. That's why different people have different stressors. One person's stressor may not affect another person in the same way. You may react negatively to that late employee, but another manager may choose to ignore the behavior.

Your reaction to the stressor can be positive or negative. That late employee is a stressor, and your reaction engendered negative feelings and a negative action. An event such as a wedding can be also be a stressor, but this time your feelings might be joy and anticipation that lead to a positive action—you go shopping for a gift for the happy couple.

Stress can be positive or negative. When people talk about stress, they're usually talking about negative stress. In fact, stress can be either positive or negative. Your reaction and the subsequent feelings determine whether you are experiencing positive or negative stress. If you are feeling excitement, anticipation, happiness, empowerment, and confidence, you're experiencing good stress, also called *eustress*. When you're feeling unhappy, worried, nervous, angry, upset, and powerless, you're experiencing bad stress, or *distress*.

You cannot live without stress. Without stress, you would be dead. Stress gets you up in the morning, gives you the impetus to meet a deadline, fills you with anticipation of a special event, and adds zest to your life. The secret to stress management is to achieve a balance between good and bad stress. When you meet every stressor with a negative reaction, you're courting burnout. At the other end of the spectrum, when you try to avoid all stress, you are approaching rust out. Neither is a good place to be.

THE PRICE YOU PAY FOR STRESS

God has created you to live in this world and prepared you to cope with all that you encounter in your day. Originally, a human's stressors were part of the daily struggle to survive, so the human body was made to deal with those stressors. When one of your prehistoric ancestors ran up against a tiger in the forest, two options presented themselves: fight or flight. In either case, the body prepared for the choice with a stress response. The body was flooded with adrenaline, which in turn revved up the body systems. The senses of sight, hearing, and smell became more acute; the heartbeat quickened; the muscles tightened; the breath shortened. Whichever choice that ancestor made, the body was ready to implement it. Once the danger was past—either the ancestor successfully ran away or successfully fought the danger—the body responses returned to normal.

Today, with the myriad of stressors that present themselves, your body often goes through a negative stress response a thousand times a day, even though there's no physical threat to you. It is impossible for the body to survive the onslaught of adrenaline over and over again, so the body has adapted. The employee coming in late didn't threaten your physical safety, yet your reaction was one of negative stress. Compound that with the argument you had at the breakfast table, the driver who cut you off on the way to work, the meeting that was canceled without notice, the stain you noticed on the front of your jacket, the new project that landed on your desk, the empty coffee pot in the break room, the performance review coming up this afternoon, the missed telephone call from a client, the employee who wants to discuss the vacation schedule, the breakdown of a critical piece of machinery, the deadline change on a report . . . the toll of negative stress grows daily.

Your body pays the price for this psychological stress. Both good and bad events can start this reaction: for example, the night before your wedding or the day you lose your job. When you find an event stressful, your body undergoes a series of changes called the stress response. At first, your body releases adrenaline, your heart beats faster, and you start to breathe more quickly. This can happen to you many times during your day.

The physical reaction follows: your heart pounds, your breathing becomes shallow, your muscles tense, your stomach contracts, your head starts throbbing, your mouth goes dry; you shiver or tremble; you grind your teeth; your eyes well up with tears; you feel dizzy or disoriented; your face freezes; your hair stands on end; you break out in a sweat; or you forget what you wanted to say.

Then your body begins to release stored sugars and fats from its resources. At this stage, you will feel driven, pressured, and tired. You may drink more coffee, eat more or less, and sleep less. If you don't resolve your stress, your body's need for energy will become greater than its ability to produce it, and you'll become chronically stressed.

You pay the price mentally as you find it more and more challenging to think clearly. You may undergo personality changes; become irritable, withdrawn, or unhappy; experience insomnia and anxiety attacks.

You pay the price physically and may develop a serious illness such as heart disease, ulcers, or cancer.

You also pay the price spiritually as you find yourself feeling more and more distanced from the center of your faith. The more stressed you become, the farther away God seems. The farther away God seems, the more stressed you become. It's a vicious circle that escalates exponentially.

Breaking the Stress Cycle: A Three-Step Process

Somehow you need to stop the stress cycle before it stops you—literally. It can be done, but it requires you to become aware of what is really going on below the surface of your external stress responses. That means taking stock of the stressor—figuring out why that stressor has so much power over you and recognizing your responses to the stressor.

1. Recognize Your Stressors

What pushes your buttons? You may be able to jot down half a dozen different stressors that are currently in your life. However, it's the not-so-familiar stressors that cause the most damage. Keep a stress diary for a week. Each time you feel your distress rise and you undergo the stress response, jot down what caused you to react.

2. Evaluate Your Reaction

Ask yourself why you reacted negatively. A good technique to get to the bottom of your reaction is called "Why Five." Ask the question *why?* and then ask it four more times. It might go something like this: "Why do I get upset when Angela questions my decision?" *Because I think that*

Angela should just do what she's asked to do. "Why?" *Because I am the boss and Angela is the employee, and it looks bad if my decisions are questioned.* "Why?" *Because the rest of my employees will wonder if Angela knows more than I do.* "Why?" *Because Angela has been here longer than I have.* "Why?" *Because she has been passed over for promotion several times.* Ahh. Here's the root of the negative reaction: a fear that Angela might know more and might resent your being the manager, instead of her.

3. Recognize Your Stress Response
Most of your stress reactions are just habits. Like Pavlov's dogs, when the stressor presents itself, you react with the learned response. If you find yourself saying, "I always _____ (fill in your feelings and actions) when I encounter _____" (fill in your stressor), you have a stress response habit. What is it that you always feel and do? Do you always get angry, feel threatened, become anxious or fearful? Do you confront, withdraw, shout, cry, shake, or scream? Pinpoint exactly what is your stress response habit.

Learning to H-A-L-T

Sometimes a stressor that normally doesn't bother you will elicit an excessive reaction from you. Usually you can ignore your staff member's whiney voice and constant complaints, yet today you feel your anger rising and a sharp retort on your lips. Your reaction to a stressor is more than just a set of body responses; it's also predicated by what is going on at that moment in your life.

Try the HALT method to determine if your stress response is based on more than just the stressor. When faced with negative stress, say to yourself, "HALT!" Then ask yourself these questions.

H — *Am I hungry?* Often hunger can trigger a stress response. If the answer is yes, have a snack.

A — *Am I angry?* When you're angry at something else, it's easy to take it out on any stressor that presents itself. If the answer is yes, acknowledge what or who you're really angry at.

L — *Am I lonely?* Feeling alone and isolated makes you more vulnerable to the stressors around you. If the answer is yes, call a friend, visit with a coworker, go for lunch with the gang, or take a moment to acknowledge that you are never alone, since God has promised to always be with you.

T — *Am I tired?* Fatigue is often the catalyst for strong negative stress response reactions. If the answer is yes, take a break. Five minutes of down time is often all you need to restore your physical equilibrium. If you can't afford any down time at all, close your eyes and offer a prayer for strength.

How to Break Your Stress Response Habit

Dealing with your momentary lapses will put you back on track, but it won't break your stress habit. Most studies of how habits are formed or broken agree that it takes up to thirty days to make or break an established habit. That means for thirty consecutive days, you must consciously, daily, without fail, choose how you will react to a stressor.

Start by choosing one stressor. It's too much to deal with all your stressors at once, so choose one that is of particular concern to you. Ask God to help you decide which stressor should be dealt with. Once you have chosen a stressor, think through how you usually react. For example, if you always feel a rush of anger when you hear a particularly negative employee complaining, that rush of anger is the habit you want to break. Remember, you can't change the stressor; you can only change your reaction to the stressor.

You'll need a rubber band to wear on your wrist for the next thirty days. The rubber band is your key to becoming aware of your stress reaction habit. Because all habits are subconscious, the secret to breaking them is to bring them to the conscious or aware level.

Whenever you see, hear, or experience your chosen stressor, before you do anything else, snap that rubber band on your wrist. It should be thick enough to inflict a little pain. That momentary flicker of pain will bring your brain to an aware state. At the same time, say the five words of power:

"Let go and let God."

These five words will remind you that you are not alone in your struggle against this stressor. God is there with you, enabling you to rise above your usual stress response reactions.

"Let go and let God." It's as simple and as profound as that. By telling yourself to let go, you consciously tell your brain that you aren't going to let this stressor trigger the usual reaction. By reminding yourself that God is able to handle your stressor, you give yourself the powerful message that it's not necessary for you to react.

Then, in your mind's eye, picture a column of light, either between you and the stressor, or all around you if you're in a stressful place. This is the divine love that surrounds you, protects you, and stands between you and whatever brings you those stressful feelings of anxiety, anger, or fear. Take three deep breaths, allowing that love to fill you and erase any negative feelings that may still linger.

Do this every time you encounter the stressor you have chosen. Do it consistently for thirty days. At the end of that period, you'll find the stressor no longer has the same power over you. In fact, you won't need the rubber band, because your subconscious will now be acting on the new habit you have formed—the habit of stopping, taking three breaths, and allowing the love of God to deal with the situation.

THE REFINER'S FIRE

A silversmith will hold a piece of silver over the fire and let it heat up. The silver has to be in the middle of the fire where the flames are hottest so that all the impurities will be burned away. The refiner stays by the fire throughout the entire process, ensuring that the silver isn't destroyed by being left too long in the flames. When he can see his reflection in the silver, he knows it is ready to take out of the fire.

When you're feeling the heat of the fire—the stressors are piling up around you—remember that God is watching over you, ensuring that you will not perish in the fire. In the end, you will be a reflection of God's image for all to see.

5

ANCHORING TO GOD IN A CHANGING WORKPLACE

Decision making used to be simpler. Chocolate, vanilla, or strawberry? Ford or Chevy? Black or with cream and sugar? Now you can choose from one hundred flavors of ice cream (and the number is still growing). Myriads of car choices flood the market from basic transportation to high-tech hybrids. And if you've tried to order coffee lately, you'll know that there are many more choices than just black or with cream and sugar.

Faced with the necessity of making multiple decisions, you may find yourself in a state of FUD, a word coined to describe the *fear, uncertainty,* and *doubt* we experience while trying to integrate a change into our workplace and lives.

- You *fear* making the wrong decision or handling the new changes in a way that will harm you or your career.
- You experience *uncertainty* that your actions and decisions will be the right ones.
- You begin to *doubt* that anything you do will affect the outcome of the change positively.

In the state of FUD, you feel powerless and vulnerable in the face of the changes around you. In the state of FUD, the still, small voice of God grows faint.

CHANGES IN BUSINESS ORGANIZATIONS

Change is invading your workplace and it's accelerating. Every day brings new changes—medical, technological, and industrial. How has this whirlwind speed of change affected your workplace?

Organizational Change

You've probably noticed the sweeping changes in how corporations and companies are structured. It used to be so easy. Your first day on the job, you were shown an organizational chart. The chart told you where you were starting out and where you could go if you worked hard and remained loyal. You knew your place in the corporate universe.

Those old pyramid-style charts, with the CEO at the top and the line workers at the bottom, have all but disappeared. The CEO and the line workers are still there, but the middle layer—your layer—is missing, squashed between a growing lower level of empowered supervisors and line workers, and a smaller upper level of hands-on CEOs. When times get tough, middle management is usually the first group to feel the brunt of layoffs and downsizing. The burgeoning ranks of out-of-work middle managers attests to this fact.

FUD sets in as you wonder what will happen to you, your job, and your place in the universe.

Leadership Change

The old autocratic style of management was simple: you were the boss, and your job was to tell your employees what to do and how to do it.

Today's leadership is more democratic with a focus on multiple roles. You're expected to share information fully with your team, rather than using the old style of need-to-know information sharing.

Empowerment is the new buzzword in the workplace. Your task as a manager is to empower people by listening, coaching, mentoring, and counseling. You can involve your staff in the areas of decision making, goal setting, and planning.

You may feel uncomfortable with the idea of empowering your staff rather than managing them in the autocratic way of yesterday. Yet God empowers all of us to be whole people with personal desires, hopes, and dreams—people who think independently and have self-determination. Unlike the stern, unforgiving, and autocratic God you may have been introduced to, a loving God understands that only by empowerment of others can you become fully alive and fully human, connected beyond yourself to the divine. Just as God empowers us, gives us free will, supports us in our struggles, loves us through our mistakes, and comforts us in our sorrow, in the same way you can be a conduit of love, support, and comfort to the people around you, even within the context of the workplace.

Technological Advances

Even if you haven't seen a lot of organizational change within your company, you've probably been hit by technological change. The proliferation of personal computers throughout companies means that every employee is now faced with technology. Even if you work on the shop floor, chances are you're working with a piece of computerized equipment. Add to this the complexity of the Internet, plus the intranets and extranets of the company system, and you may feel overwhelmed by the demands made upon you to learn and master new technologies.

Older managers may remember the first time they sat in front of a computer and realized that their jobs depended on learning to operate this foreign object. What did you think of this change? Did the prospect excite you? Did you fear you wouldn't be smart enough to learn its intricacies? Did you feel angry at the company for making you leave behind your old methods, which as far as you were concerned, were perfectly fine the way they were?

Younger managers may remember the difficulties in moving from the freedom of the classroom to the constraints of the boardroom. The changes were profound: in clothing, in manners, in social interactions, in the sense of personal power. Did you feel constrained? Fearful that you wouldn't measure up? Excited by this new aspect of your working life? Annoyed that you were expected to conform to the new norms?

Technology has enabled the workplace to gather and disseminate information at a breathtaking pace. One issue of the *New York Times* now contains more information than a man or woman living in the Renaissance era would have read in an entire lifetime.[1]

Quite simply, most managers today suffer from information overload. From the media—newspapers, magazines, radio, and television—to electronic communications—e-mail, fax machines, paging systems, and cell phones; from office computers to a myriad of programs such as IM, Skype, Twitter, Facebook, and Plaxo, you're bombarded with information from every direction. Now a good deal of your day is spent in information management: *What can I use? What do I need today? What should I save in case I need it tomorrow?* Somewhere between the speed and volume of the information presented to you and its short shelf life, you must deal with the self-knowledge that you haven't quite caught up.

Paradigm Shifts

The new paradigm in the workplace is increased involvement of the whole person. You are expected to bring a personal commitment to your organization, which may take the form of:

- voluntary overtime to finish a task
- participation on special task forces or teams
- voluntary education in areas relating to your job

These expectations go against the belief that you should work to live, not live to work. Lifestyle plays an important role in the workplace as people increasingly try to find balance between a healthy home life and a successful career.

That's because the old paradigm of climbing corporate ladders and chasing dollars has shifted to an emphasis on a holistic lifestyle where work, home, and spirituality are in harmony.

The paradigm of loyalty in the workplace has changed too. Once there was a feeling of family and closeness among employees. Some companies provided company recreational opportunities, sent flowers when a family member was ill, provided generous scholarships, and generally took care of their own when times got tough. In return, you gave your company your all.

Workers once chose a company for their entire career. Today, few people remain at the same company until retirement. Today's workers see each job as a stepping-stone of experience and knowledge that leads to the next job. They don't expect to climb organizational ladders. They company-hop instead, going from one company to another until they reach the top of the profession. Even then, as CEOs, they may jump ship and take command of a competitor's vessel.

But what about the employees who don't want to company-hop—

who hope to stay with a company until retirement age? They become the unwitting victims of change.

Downsizing, reengineering, restructuring, takeovers, mergers—you read the daily horror stories of layoffs, firings, closings, and bankruptcies. There's always a story of the loyal employee who worked with the company for thirty-five years and now is unemployed.

It's no wonder so many people are in a state of FUD: the fear of losing a job, the uncertainty of moving into the job market, the doubt that they are in the right place for security.

Paradigm shifts are always frightening. All great spiritual leaders create paradigm shifts when they offer their followers new ways of thinking. Jesus created a paradigm shift when he suggested his way of life was for *everyone*, not just the good, the rich, or the titled. Many of those who heard him must have experienced FUD: fear that he was preaching anarchy, uncertainty how to follow his simple precepts, doubt that he was right.

Attitudinal Changes

Because the business world has been hit by restructuring and technology, the workplace has had its share of changes. Look around your workplace. The people are different from those of a few years ago. More women have taken on management roles, more diverse cultural mixes are seen in every department, and there is a blurring of gender roles and expectations. The old stereotypes and paradigms are gone. The boss isn't necessarily male, and the secretary isn't necessarily female. You may find yourself working with people who are light-years away from you in experience and background. These people may even be in a position of authority over you, and you must learn how to work effectively with them.

There is also an acceptance of negativity in the workplace. At one time, no one felt free to express dissatisfaction with the company or its employees. To do so might put a job in jeopardy. Not so today when negativity can be rampant and some meetings end in a gripe-and-whine session.

The problems begin when you attempt to deal with change by trying to put it into a box of either *what was* or *what should be*. Change doesn't fit into either of these boxes. Change is *what is*. Change is a present reality.

Here's what happens when you try to put change into a box.

You receive a memo from the executive office outlining a restructuring of your department. You'll now be part of a larger team made up of people from several other departments. Your employees have been reassigned and will no longer report to you. You won't be reporting to the same boss anymore. In fact, your reporting will now be part of a team report, rather than an individual one. Your performance will be measured by the success of the team.

When you meet your new team, you're shocked to see that your old boss is one of the members, as is one of your former subordinates. The rest are all new faces.

You sit through the first two meetings saying little. You're more and more aware of a growing discomfort with the group, and you know that you're not giving a very good account of yourself either. You wonder what your former boss is thinking. Does she report to others? You don't know. You don't like the way your former subordinate feels free to criticize anything he doesn't like. You wonder how he has the nerve to do that when you're there.

The initial excitement you felt when you heard of your appointment to the team soon dissipates. Now disappointment sets in as the reality of the situation overwhelms what you thought was going to be an exciting, career-boosting change. You keep thinking back to the way it was. You did your job. They did theirs. Things got done. Why fix what wasn't broken?

The team leader keeps telling you why the self-directed team was put in place, but you can see that it is not working the way it should. It should be effective. It should be powerful. It should be a decision-making entity. But it isn't.

Eventually you find yourself picking up on the negatives of the team, pointing out failures and mistakes, jumping on errors. You keep reminding the others of how badly the team is doing, how much better everything was before. Before long, they begin to see your point of view, and soon most of the meetings are no more than complaining sessions.

The trouble is, you don't know where to go from here. You're stuck, and there's nothing you can do about it. You're in FUD.

A reality check allows you to make decisions based on the nature of the change, *right now*. It gives you the power to overcome the FUD and take control of the change. Here's how it works:

Step 1: Look at the way it was. What was it like before this change took place? List both the pros and cons for this state. Be honest and realistic in your assessment of how it used to be. Don't be tempted to see past events as better than they really were.

Step 2: Look at the way it is supposed to be. What was supposed to happen with this change? What was the reason for the change and how was the change supposed to address this? Don't look at what has happened, but instead look at what was supposed to happen.

Step 3: Look at the way it really is. Here's your chance to figure out where you are now. Be realistic. What's working? What isn't? What's really happening with the change? What are the effects of this change on people, on structures, on you? Remember, the key here is to be realistic. Try to avoid the negative. Simply state the facts, as they are, not as they should be or as you'd like them to be.

Once you've made your reality-check assessment, you're ready to make decisions regarding this change. Take the earlier example of the self-directed team member.

The reality is:

- I know some of the team members.
- I don't know other team members.
- My performance appraisal is based on the team's success.
- The performance appraisal of the others is also based on the team's success.
- If we succeed at our project, we all win.
- If we fail, we all fail.

Based on this assessment, it becomes clear that any decisions you make should ensure the success of the team. If you make a decision that doesn't lead to the success of the team—the decision not to be involved, for example—you will prevent this change from taking you where you want to go.

How Do You Deal with Change?

Just how fast is the world changing? Before 1940 there was no polyester, cellophane tape, credit cards, or Internet. Nor did we have refrigerator/freezers, personal computers, jet travel, or antibiotics. Humankind had not yet walked on the moon, invented the atomic bomb, or patented a birth-control pill.

In 1990, within one year, the Berlin Wall crumbled, the USSR disintegrated, and the Cold War ended. In the '90s the world saw incredible progress in genetics, including the first cloned animal. In the '90s, the Internet boomed from an esoteric information highway for government and educational institutions to a household information-and-entertainment source. In the '90s, Viagra made its debut, heralding the desire of those aging baby boomers to hang on to their youth!

Our new century is fraught with change. In just a few short years, we've seen economies boom and bust, and stock markets soar and plummet. Family structures, moral values, and societal attitudes—all are changing.

Change is accelerating. When you consider how Jules Verne's 1873 classic *Around the World in Eighty Days* was considered impossible fiction, and today, the space shuttle can orbit the earth in eighty-one minutes, you begin to realize the mind-boggling speed of change in our society.

To get a feeling for this accelerating change, try squeezing 50,000 years of human history into 50 years. If that were possible, here is how it would look:

50 years ago	time of the caveman
5 years ago	communications with history (cave drawings)
6 months ago	invention of the printing press
1 month ago	invention of the electric light
3 weeks ago	the Wright Brothers' first flight
1½ weeks ago	first television set sold
yesterday	the Berlin Wall fell

The last few days of such a time line would reflect 90 percent of the technology affecting us today!

How do you cope with this kind of whirlwind? How are you handling the FUD? Take this simple quiz to discover your FUD Profile.

DISCOVER YOUR FUD (FEAR, UNCERTAINTY, DOUBT) PROFILE

Directions: Circle the letter of each statement with which you agree. Your responses are not meant to indicate whether you like or dislike change, but how you respond when the going gets tough and FUD sets in.

1.
   A. When someone suggests something new, I find it hard to know how to make it work.
   B. If I hang in long enough, the change will eventually run its course and I won't have to deal with it.
   C. Most change is inherently negative, and the Pollyannas who insist on seeing it with rose-colored glasses are in for a shock.
   D. I don't understand why people are always trying to change things when there's nothing wrong with what we have.
   E. I just go with the flow. There's nothing I can do to stop or affect or control the change.

2.
   A. If I don't like the change that's going on, I point out how much better things were before the change was introduced, or how the change isn't measuring up to what was expected to happen.
   B. I think I'm entitled to be left alone. I've done my share of changing.
   C. Too many contradictory expectations come attached to change. I never know what's expected of me.
   D. I know what I do well, and I know what works. I don't need to go through a lot of change.
   E. I often wish that I were more tuned in to the changes around me so that I could use them to my advantage.

3.
   A. I'm not good at handling change. I second-guess myself all the time and feel really negative about what is happening around me.
   B. If I'm dealing with a change that makes me feel inadequate, I work harder than most others to make the change work.

C. When I hear that there are going to be changes in my workplace, I try to keep a low profile. That way, no one will bother me.

D. I get worried when I see all the changes in the workplace today because I know that the old methods work best in business.

E. When change occurs, I usually feel out of control and powerless. I worry about where it will take me.

4.

A. I'm probably the only person who takes time to assess the downside of all the changes that are going on around me.

B. Change is just doing the same old thing with a different spin on it. Nothing is really new in the workplace. I know—I've been around awhile.

C. In my experience, most change is negative, just a knee-jerk reaction to something that would have righted itself if left alone.

D. I'm tired of people telling me to think outside the box when dealing with change. I don't know what's so wrong with being in the box!

E. I always wait to see what the change will bring before I do anything about it, even though I may get left behind while others forge ahead with the change.

When done, count the number of As, Bs, Cs, Ds, and Es that you circled.

A _____
B _____
C _____
D _____
E _____

To which letter or letters did you respond most frequently? You'll probably find that you agreed with several statements in the same category, or it may be that you're all over the map when it comes to dealing with FUD. Whatever your score, by looking at the underlying meaning behind each set of responses, you'll be able to determine where you need to address the FUD in your life.

If you agreed mostly with A statements: You may have difficulty with change, because you find yourself continually harking back to how much better you thought things were before the change. You may focus on how the change isn't working, and as a result, become negative in the face of change. If you feel you've lost control, you'll begin to spread negativity throughout the workplace.

If you agreed mostly with B statements: You may react to change in one of two ways: either you feel that you have to react to every change that comes your way, or you choose to ignore all change. The resulting FUD from either of these extreme reactions paralyzes you. You may try too hard, believing that you have to impress those around you. You come in early, stay late, and keep your nose to the grindstone. Or you simply pretend to be working on the change when, in fact, you're busy sabotaging the change. Rather than embracing all, or resisting all, you need to learn how to be more discriminating—how to separate the urgent from the important and the trivial from the monumental.

If you agreed mostly with C statements: You may see change as a threat. For you, change usually means that you will lose something, rather than gain something. FUD sets in because you're distrustful of change, often seeing the change as a plot for others to usurp your power or control. Usually, this comes from your belief that all change is inherently dangerous. As well, you find it hard to meet the expectations that come with change and end up trying to please everyone. You need to learn how to go with the flow when dealing with change.

If you agreed mostly with D statements: You may choose to stay inside the boxes of what is known in order to protect yourself from the frightening unknowns of change. You cling to the way you always have done it, closing yourself off from any possibilities that may be created by the change. Your goal is to maintain the status quo at all costs.

If you agreed mostly with E statements: You're like a boat on the ocean of change with no rudder, no engine, and no sail. You allow the change to blow you this way and that and often find yourself beached on a shore that isn't what you wanted or expected. The resulting FUD leaves you feeling helpless and hopeless. To avoid heading in the wrong direction, you need to learn how to use the change to reach your goals.

THE FOUR PHASES OF THE CHANGE PROCESS

When you're faced with change that seems threatening, your response will fall into a four-step process. How long you spend at each stage depends upon how strongly you feel about the change, either negatively or positively, and how important it is for you to assimilate the change.

First Phase: Denial

"No! Not me! There's no way I'm going to do that!" Sound familiar? That's the typical first reaction when a change is encountered.

Second Phase: Resistance

When it becomes obvious that the change is not going away and that you will have to deal with it, resistance sets in. Resistance comes from fear. When you perceive that the change will affect your comfort zone in some way, you begin to fear it. Your resistance can take the form of loud vocal protests, specific actions aimed against the change, or passive nonparticipation.

Third Phase: Acceptance
When resistance fails, acceptance sets in. This is usually a brief period in which you realize that you're going to have to deal with the change, regardless of your personal feelings toward it.

Final Phase: Integration
Now it's time to make that change part of your life. You begin to learn how to use the new telephone system. You accept the new way of conducting staff reviews. You join the task force on employee relations. The change that caused you to fear soon becomes a way of life, and it's hard to imagine how you got along before the change.

THIS TOO WILL PASS
"Plus ça change, plus c'est la même chose." The more things change, the more they remain the same, an old French adage tells us. In other words, when things stop changing, then things are different. This is a paradox that philosophers love to explore.

As a business professional, you have better things to do than explore paradoxes. But you do need to see that your present state of change is simply that—a state that comes, is, and then passes. If change is constant, then whatever state of change you're in today will eventually give way to another.

- The new software you have to learn to use will eventually be replaced by even newer software.
- The latest reorganization will give way to another reorganization.
- The self-directed team will be reassigned.
- You will move on to another job.

The breathtaking changes that may seem overwhelming right now will, in time, pass on. New things will come, and they too will pass.

The change you experience now will soon undergo transformation. You can be part of that transformation. The decisions you make based upon your reality check make you a catalyst for positive change. This takes you beyond FUD into a state of movement and flux.

"Change and decay in all around I see. O Thou who changest not, abide with me."[2] So goes the old hymn, and in these words is the bedrock paradox upon which you can live with change: God does not change; God does not leave you; God can bring good from any change in your life.

6

FINDING FREEDOM IN GOD'S UNLIMITED TIME

There just aren't enough hours in the day!" That's a common complaint of managers, probably one you've made many times. In your rush-rush, do-do, hurry-hurry life, time is the enemy, one you battle daily as you try to squeeze your long to-do list into the twenty-four hours at your disposal. You may be on the job only eight hours a day—just 33 percent of your time, but it seems as if 99 percent of the work must be done in those few hours.

Because so much time is lost by time wasters, you may have adopted irrational beliefs about time to make up for your lack of time control.

FOUR IRRATIONAL BELIEFS ABOUT TIME

1. There's not enough time.
There's always enough time. Time is an infinite quantity. After this second comes another, and after this minute, another one. After this day, another day, and after this year, another year. From century to century, eon to eon, millennium to millennium, time is never-ending. The psalmist got it right

when he said, "For a thousand years in your [God's] sight are like a day that has just gone by" (Ps. 90:4, NIV). That certainly puts the thought that time is limited into perspective. Time is a divine gift—limitless and beyond counting.

2. I have to save time.

This irrational belief presupposes that time is a commodity that can, like a penny, be put away and saved for use later on. It is as if you have a time bank into which you can pour those few precious minutes you saved this morning by skipping breakfast, or that hour you had on hand yesterday when the morning meeting was canceled. Then, when you're feeling pressed for time, you just withdraw those minutes or that extra hour and use it as you need it. It doesn't work that way. Time will be, time is, and time passes. Once a moment has passed, it is irretrievable.

> WHEN YOUR CLOCK IS TICKING AND YOU REALIZE THAT THERE WON'T BE ENOUGH TIME TO COMPLETE YOUR PROJECT, ASK GOD TO GIVE YOU THE TIME YOU NEED FOR THE TASK.

Only God can "save" time. When your clock is ticking and you realize that there won't be enough time to complete your project, ask God to give you the time you need for the task. Often that small prayer will take away the stress of trying to get it done. Instead you'll be able to work with a sense of timelessness that allows you to be more efficient, more focused, and more productive.

3. I'll get more done if I work longer.

Unfortunately, this isn't true. You've probably already discovered that there seems to be a point beyond which you are no longer working effectively. If you were one of those students who tried to pull an all-nighter before a big exam, you know that your ability to retain information decreased with the amount of time you spent studying. In fact, more is done in short bursts of time. God's work is done in God's time, and only God knows how much time that is.

4. I have to get time under control.
This implies that time is like a new puppy—raw and untrained. All it takes is a little discipline, a little effort, and you'll be the master. Time is a concept, nothing more. How can you control something that is ephemeral, fleeting, without substance or shape? It's only the tyranny of the clock that holds you in bondage. Have you become a time fanatic, building time management spreadsheets, creating priority folders and lists, color coding tasks, and separating paperwork into multiple priority piles?

You cannot control time. Time controls you—if you let it. When you reach the point where you can believe that your time belongs to God, you can let go of the need to be in control. When you begin your day by offering up your time to God, you give yourself perfect freedom.

These irrational beliefs about time management may lead to some of your issues with time in your workday. However, there is also the psychological side of your time management skills to consider. Different people deal with time in different ways. Your psychological obstacles may be the primary reasons you procrastinate; have trouble saying no, delegating, or making time management decisions.

WHAT IS YOUR TIME STYLE?

Directions: Underline all of the words in the four columns that describe how you feel or react toward time and time issues. You can choose as many or as few words as apply to you, from any of the columns.

A	B	C	D
Confident	Efficient	Indecisive	Thorough
Impatient	Organized	Impractical	Meticulous
Reactive	Fast-paced	Disorganized	Practical
Impulsive	Goal-oriented	Multitasking	Task-oriented
Last-minute	Schedules	What time is it?	Logical
Now-oriented	Sequential	Whenever	Timetables
I'll find time	Future-oriented	Someday	Pressured
Deadline stress	Right away	Scattered	Don't rush me
Close enough	Do it right	What deadline?	Exactly right
Always tomorrow	Do it faster	Always next week	Controlled
Urgent	Tough	Random	Accurate
Free-and-easy	I plan time	Can't say no	Stick to the schedule
Go with the flow	Excellence	Good enough	Perfectionist
Great	Do it now	Unsure	Could be better
I'll get others	I'll direct others	Let's work together	I'll do it myself

Count the number of words you chose from each column.

A _____

B _____

C _____

D _____

From which column did you choose the most words?

If most of your choices are from column A, your time challenges are these: You tend to leave things to the last minute and then get caught by deadline pressures. You do your best work when under a time crunch. You have a tendency to jump in without too much thought and often get caught with too many things on your plate. However, you're not constrained by a desire to do it perfectly but are willing to do it well enough.

Others may see you as someone who doesn't understand how important it is to get things done, since you have an easygoing attitude toward time.

If most of your choices are from column B, your time challenges are these: You like to be in control of the situation and find it difficult when other people make changes that affect your time lines. You are good at directing others and can see the big picture when it comes to setting priorities and deadlines. You like to have things organized and mapped out, with ultimate goals in mind. You dislike having to wait. Others may see you as controlling and bossy, sometimes inflexible and demanding when it comes to dealing with time.

If most of your choices are from column C, your time challenges are these: Your inability to say no is your greatest time challenge. You usually have a myriad of things going on at once and find it hard to devote time to just one of them. You prefer to work with others on projects, but you may be disorganized and scattered in your approach. You find it difficult to make decisions about your time priorities. Others may see you as spacey, out of control, even impractical as you extravagantly promise all things to all people.

If most of your choices are from column D, your time challenges are these: You don't like deadline pressures. You prefer to have ample time to do a project and do it well. You find it difficult to settle for less than perfect. You can become bogged down in a project by paralysis of analysis because you have a need to weigh all factors and considerations before making a decision. People may see you as being too picky, demanding more time than others, and wasting time going over the work of others to make sure it is up to your high standards.

Each person is an individual and expresses himself or herself differently, and that includes how that person views time. Problems arise in the workplace when someone who tends to leave things to the last minute works with someone who likes to plan ahead and ensure ample time to complete a project. When the person who wants to control the schedule meets up with the person who just can't stick to a schedule, problems arise and sparks fly.

As a mindful manager, your only recourse is to consciously put your time in God's hands. Only then can you hope to restore harmony in a workplace disrupted by time issues. Only then can you focus on being present in the moment, and not on the clock.

Regardless of your time-management style, you'll probably be facing the same time issues as everyone else. The only difference is in the way you handle them.

Four Daily Time Thieves

It'ss not the big things that destroy the sense of order in your life but the daily time thieves that enter your workplace. Which of these time robbers do you experience?

1. Disorganization

- Do you lose things on your desk?
- Do you frequently rummage through file drawers looking for files?
- Do you take work home and forget to bring it back?

2. Doing Too Little

- Do you often feel like you don't know where to start or which task to do next?
- Does it seem like your to-do list never gets done?
- Do you have an overflowing in-box on your desk and a backed-up e-mail in-box?
- Do you feel like you waste time just trying to sort out what to do next?

3. Doing Too Much
- Do you work on many major projects at once?
- Do you have a dozen little things that need doing, that you could do in less than half an hour if you could just get to them?
- Do you have trouble saying no?

4. Procrastinating
- Do you put off important tasks over and over?
- Do you wait until you are in the right mood before you begin a task?
- Do you believe that the task will become easier later on?
- Do you hope that the task will go away if you wait long enough?

Do these daily thieves rob you of time? They undermine your ability to get things done, reduce your productivity, and force you to suffer the tyranny of the clock. Here are some remedies for the four time wasters.

Disorganized? Declutter!
Is your workspace cluttered? For one day, try to put everything you touch in its place. Do that again tomorrow and the next day. Pretty soon organizing will become a habit. It takes little time to put each thing away when finished, and the habit will save you time in the long run.

Or at the end of each day, pick *five* things that have accumulated on your desk and *stow or throw*. Delete five unneeded computer files. Doing a little each day will be easier than tackling the mess all at once.

Doing Too Little? Take Control!
Have you noticed how often the same piece of paper in your in-box gets handled over and over? It's another form of procrastination that is easily remedied.

Pick up the first piece of paper in your in-box. Don't look at it in terms of how you *feel* about that specific task, instruction, order, memo, or information. Instead ask these four D questions:

1. *Dump?* Can you dump this piece of paper? If you throw it away, will it make any difference? Why are you keeping it? If you can't think of a good reason, then get rid of it. If the answer is, "No, I can't dump it," then ask . . .

2. *Delay?* Can you delay action on this piece of paper until a later date? If you can, put it in a tickler file. A tickler file has slots for each day of the month, plus eleven additional ones for the months of the year. Decide when you're going to handle this piece of paper and put it in the appropriate slot. (Each morning, if you take a few minutes to go through the papers for that day in your tickler file, you can use the same four-D system to handle them.) If you can't delay the piece of paper, ask . . .

3. *Delegate?* Is there someone to whom you can delegate this task? If there is, do so now. Not later—now. You may have to stop to make a phone call, walk to another desk, or send an e-mail, but do it. Don't put it off until later. If you have no one to whom to delegate this particular piece of paper, then . . .

4. *Do.* That's right. Do it. Now. Before you go to the next piece of paper. It's a daunting thought, because it means stopping everything else and handling the piece of paper. However, once it's done, it's gone from your in-box and you're ready to move to the next piece of paper and repeat the process.

You can use the same system to deal with the piles of e-mail that you've saved in your in-box on your computer.

Doing Too Much? Just Say No!

Decide what you must do and what you want to do, and say no to everything else. Spend time prayerfully contemplating the requests that come to you. Most people don't like doing tedious or difficult jobs. If they can pass them to you, they will. If you're cooperative, you'll find your time filled with irrelevant tasks. You'll be extremely busy but fail to do your own job. Be firm. If the task is not something you need to do to support your other tasks, say no.

Procrastinating? JDI!

In a nutshell, you procrastinate when you put off things that you should be focusing on right now, usually in favor of doing something that is more enjoyable or that you're more comfortable doing.

A common cause of procrastination is feeling overwhelmed by the task. You may not know where to begin. Or you may doubt that you have the skills or resources you need, so you seek comfort in doing tasks you know you're capable of completing. Unfortunately, the big task won't go away—truly important tasks rarely do. JDI—Just do it.

COMMON TIME CHALLENGES

Despite all that you may be doing to take control of time in your day, there are other time challenges that can still trip you up.

1. Trying to Eat an Elephant

When a large project lands on your desk, it's like an elephant sitting there. All you can think of is how much time it will take. If it comes with a tight deadline, you feel your stress level rising.

Never try to eat an elephant all at once. In your mind, the task might be a big, vague, messy notion. Plot the task. Put it on paper to make it clear, more tangible, doable. This puts it in focus and makes the project more manageable. When you do this, you usually find there's less to do than you thought.

Break the job into smaller pieces. "Inform everyone on the customer list of the time change for ordering new parts," can become "Call five customers before lunch." Don't say, "I've got to get that project done," say, "Today I will outline part 1." When you do a small, manageable task, you feel good about it and better about the project in general.

Work through a big project in a step-by-step manner. Once you break the big task into small steps, clear them all from your desk except one. This could be the first step, or one of the other less-intimidating steps. Do it. Start now, not after lunch, or after you have cleaned your desk drawer. Dive in and do it. Work for ten minutes solid. In that time, you'll make some progress. After ten hardworking minutes, stop. Look at what you've accomplished, and decide if you're going to quit or carry on. If you feel like quitting, quit. If you see it isn't so bad after all, use the momentum you've gained. Keep going. Finish that step. Put it away. Take out another step. Do it.

Keeping only one step at a time on your desk helps reduce the overwhelming feeling you have about this task.

2. Putting Bowling Balls in a Box

Imagine you have a box, enough bowling balls to fill it, some tennis balls, and some golf balls. The box is the time allotted to you in your working day. The bowling balls are the important or urgent projects that you know are going to take a lot of time. The tennis balls are the less time-demanding projects. The golf balls are those myriad of little things that you have to get done in a day. Chances are, unless you put the bowling balls in first, you won't have room to fit them all in.

It follows that we plan time slots for our big issues before anything else, or the inevitable golf ball and tennis ball issues will fill up our days and we won't have room for the big issues. (A big issue doesn't necessarily have to be a work task—it could be your child's sports day or a lunch with friends.)

3. The Deadline High
Some people love coming up against a tight deadline. Working against a deadline can bring strong rushes of adrenaline. You may delay a job to experience this rush of adrenaline, but you may fail to finish that job because you left it until too late. The way to avoid deadline-high procrastination is to set intermediate goals. Many small deadlines allow you to have some deadline highs without jeopardizing the whole project.

4. The 80/20 Rule
Do you spend your days in a frenzy of activity but achieve very little? It may be because you're not concentrating your effort on the things that matter the most.

Italian economist Vilfredo Pareto studied land ownership and discovered that 80 percent of the land in Italy (and other countries) was owned by 20 percent of the population. He studied other parameters and discovered the same rule held. For example: 80 percent of the wealth was held by 20 percent of the people, and 80 percent of the livestock was owned by 20 percent of the people. Although this is called the 80/20 rule, the figures are not exact but serve as a rule of thumb to remind you that things are not distributed evenly.

The 80/20 rule holds true in other areas, such as management.

- In sales, 20 percent of the agents make 80 percent of the sales.
- In management, 20 percent of employees generate 80 percent of the problems.

- Eighty percent of managerial time is spent dealing with 20 percent of the employees.
- Twenty percent of the workers do 80 percent of the work.
- Eighty percent of unfocused effort generates 20 percent of the results.
- Twenty percent of focused effort achieves 80 percent of the results.
- Eighty percent of the work is accomplished in the first 20 percent of the time spent on a task.

Although these figures may not be exact, there is no doubt that a small number of sales reps sell the most, or that just a few employees cause the most personnel issues. The time management aim is to concentrate effort on the 20 percent of tasks that produce 80 percent of the results. Do the high-payoff tasks first and then work on the rest.

The discussion of time management becomes moot when you realize that you have no time at all except this moment. The past is gone. The future has yet to come. The divine gift to you is this moment. No more, no less. For many, this is a frightening thought, but for those with faith in God, this is pure freedom. It means that the only time you have to worry about is now.

If, in this moment, you are mindful of God, then what happens next is not important. The next moment, when it comes, is all that need concern you. And the moment after that, and the moment after that.

If no more moments are allotted to you, then in this moment, being mindful of God means there will be no regrets, no if only's, just the complete assurance that you have used this moment as it was meant to be used.

PART THREE

WORKING WITH OTHERS

YOU PROBABLY HAVE DAYS when you think you have the greatest job in the world—if it weren't for the other people! Working with others isn't easy, even if you're in a compatible workplace with like-minded individuals. You will always experience times when communication breaks down, when tempers flare, and when God seems far away from the turmoil around you.

If ever there was an opportunity to connect with God in your workplace, it is in your capacity as a manager of other people. But what if those other people have a negative attitude, or are hard to understand, difficult to work with, and disinterested in doing their jobs? That's when it is most important to remain mindful of God's presence.

Communication is more than words; empowering others means more than giving them free rein; and handling conflict involves more than writing up a report for an employee's file. When these aspects of the manager's role are carried out with a sense of the divine being with you, and a true commitment to remaining mindful of God, you'll find your interaction with people in your workplace easier.

7

CONNECTING WITH OTHERS IN A GOD-CENTERED WAY

A good job used to mean a full-time, permanent position with good pay and benefits. Today people want more than pay and perks; they want good-quality relationships with their employer and with other employees. Good relationships in the workplace are as important to job satisfaction as pay or benefits. They are, in fact, the key ingredient of a good job.

When employees can't find quality relationships in the workplace, they often seek other jobs. When that's impossible, ongoing weak relationships result in low morale and absenteeism. As a manager, you play an integral role in promoting and maintaining the quality relationships in your department. It is up to you.

You may be feeling daunted by the idea of bringing harmony into a disharmonious group, but realize that discord is part of human nature. The Israelites, traveling through the wilderness to the Promised Land, argued and fought among themselves. The disciples of Jesus, even though they witnessed astounding events, still found time to squabble and argue.

How are the relationships in the group you manage? Is there more discord than harmony? Is the emphasis on teamwork rather than on a "lone wolf" mentality? Do people respect each other? Do they respect your management role?

YOUR RELATIONSHIP INVENTORY

How do you connect with the people you manage? Circle Y (Yes) or N (No) for each question.

Communication

1. Do those you manage frequently share their thoughts and ideas with you? Y or N
2. Do you openly share your ideas, thoughts, and feelings with others? Y or N
3. Do the people you work with listen to one another? Y or N

Conflict

1. Can you tell people when you're feeling angry or hurt? Y or N
2. When resolving conflict, does a win/win attitude prevail? Y or N
3. Do you and others discuss conflicts openly? Y or N

Care and Respect

1. Do you feel your team members respect you? Y or N
2. Do you openly show your respect and care for others? Y or N
3. Do you feel valued by others? Y or N

Your Role

1. Are you comfortable with your role as a manager of this group? Y or N
2. Are you satisfied with how those you supervise respond to you as their manager? Y or N

3. Do you feel that you have control in how you carry out your management duties? Y or N

Scoring: Count the number of yes answers and no answers you marked and write them here: Yes _____ No _____. The number of yes answers indicates the degree of good relationships in your workplace. If you have more no answers, there are probably some relationship issues you need to address.

The workplace is a jumble of many different personalities. What sets the workplace apart from many other places is that everyone, even the difficult people, must cooperate in order to be productive. With so many differences among people—age, gender, religion, race, ethnic background, and culture—the challenges you face as a manager are much more complex than just getting along. As well, many people are dealing with emotional problems, medical problems, or mental problems, or may be taking medication that adversely affects their behavior. The mindful manager tries to understand what could be going on in employees' lives outside of work that could influence their behavior at work.

WHY DO YOU REACT TO DIFFICULT PEOPLE?

You have hot buttons that, when pushed, cause you to react. A hot button can be a number of things: a word, a sound, a facial expression, a phrase, or a smell. You've experienced pleasant feelings when you hear a special song, or unpleasant, if that song reminds you of a painful time. The smell of baking bread triggers memories for many. And so do certain words, facial expressions, even phrases. Most hot buttons are unconscious—you don't know what they are, and you're not aware when they are pushed. "I don't know why, but I just don't trust that guy," you may say.

Often you label people "difficult" because they've pushed one of your hot buttons—they've triggered a negative reaction within you. That hot button usually is simply a result of a personality difference. What the difficult person sees as reasonable and acceptable behavior you may see as obnoxious and obstructive behavior.

Humans are wonderful, diverse, infinitely different beings, created by God to live on this earth. Yet that diversity brings much conflict to the workplace. Because you and your employees may have a different orientation toward how you interact with each other and how you perform your work, conflict and misunderstanding can arise.

WHO ARE YOUR DIFFICULT PEOPLE?

Behavior Types: The SPOT Profile—Self, Process, Others, Task
There are two basic types of people: task-oriented and people-oriented. Each dominant type has two subtypes. For the task-oriented people, there are those who just want to get it done (process) and those who want to get it right (task). People-oriented people are usually either "I like you" (self) types or "you like me" (others) types.

You can use the Behavior Orientation Chart on page 111 to assess your own type and then assess the types of the people with whom you need to communicate. Here's how:

1. First, find out what type of person you are by completing the Personal Behavior Orientation Analysis on the next page.

2. Apply the same test to people you have conflict with. If you don't want to ask them to take the test, you should know enough about their work habits and styles to answer the questions in a general way. Some managers use this test as an icebreaker for a staff meet-

ing. Most people like to find out their work types and enjoy seeing how their coworkers rank.

3. Use your knowledge of their behavior orientation to communicate with your difficult people in a way they will understand.

Remember, you don't have to change yourself; just be more aware of yourself and aware of, and in tune with, the other person. Also, being aware that people have different ways of looking at a situation will help you be more empathetic and more observant as you negotiate.

PERSONAL BEHAVIOR ORIENTATION ANALYSIS

Directions: In each pair of characteristics below, check one that best describes your behavior. Total all the checks in column A. Do not add up column B.

Column A		Column B
_____ Direct	or	_____ Indirect
_____ Talkative	or	_____ Quiet
_____ Confronting	or	_____ Avoiding
_____ Goes after things	or	_____ Waits for things
_____ Demonstrative	or	_____ Thoughtful
_____ Leader	or	_____ Follower
_____ Active	or	_____ Passive
_____ Adventurous	or	_____ Timid
_____ Demanding	or	_____ Accepting
_____ Intense	or	_____ Relaxed
_____ **Total**		**No Total**

Do the same for the pairs below in columns C and D. Total all the checks in column C. Do not add up the checks in column D.

Column C

		Column D
_____ Friendly	or	_____ Standoffish
_____ Sentimental	or	_____ Analytical
_____ Outgoing	or	_____ Reserved
_____ Extroverted	or	_____ Introverted
_____ Dramatic	or	_____ Restrained
_____ Interested in people	or	_____ Interested in things
_____ Sociable	or	_____ Lone wolf
_____ Spontaneous	or	_____ Methodical
_____ Impulsive	or	_____ Deliberate
_____ Sympathetic	or	_____ Detached
_____ **Total**		**No Total**

Enter your total from column A on the Behavior Orientation Chart on the next page by putting a dot on the appropriate number of the vertical **Task/Relationship Orientation** line. Do the same on the horizontal **Self/Others Orientation** line for your total from column C.

Draw a line joining the two dots across the triangular area between them. It will go across the orientation area that describes your behavior type.

Behavior Orientation Chart

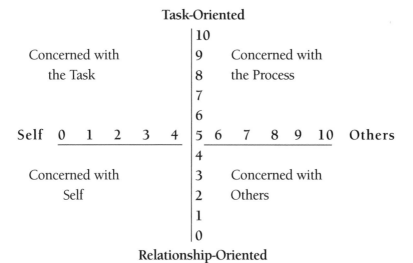

The closer your score is to the number 5 on both lines, the more balanced or mixed your type.

Example: A total of 9 As (vertical line) joined with a total of 7 Cs (horizontal line) indicates that you are task-oriented but you want others to like you. However, a reading of 4 As and 6 Cs says that you like to be liked but won't force yourself on others.

If your readings are very definitive, you don't have to make yourself over. Simply know your characteristics and adjust your behavior a little more drastically when you are with certain people in crucial situations. For example, if you know that your focus is on the task and getting it done, remember that others in the group may require some relationship building before they are willing to commit to the task.

Concerned with *Self* (lower left-hand quadrant): Self-oriented people are less patient and more competitive. They express their opinions readily and like to contribute to the discussion. Gregarious and outgoing, they display natural leadership ability and creativity. The most important thing for them is to be *the center of attention*.

Concerned with *Process* (upper right-hand quadrant): Process-oriented people are also less patient and more competitive. However, they tend to be autocratic, dictatorial, and less inclined to discuss. They need to feel in control. The most important thing for them is to *get the job done*.

Concerned with *Others* (lower right-hand quadrant): Other-oriented people are patient and cooperative. They usually reserve their opinions unless asked, and seldom contribute to the discussion. The most important thing for them is to *have everyone like them*.

Concerned with *Task* (upper left-hand quadrant): Task-oriented people are reserved and unlikely to contribute to discussions. They prefer to work alone on a task and don't like to be rushed or have deadlines change. They like parameters and guidelines for the task. The most important thing for them is *get the job done right*.

WHERE DOES CONFLICT ARISE IN THE SPOT PROFILE?

Some Common Conflict Areas

In general, task-oriented people (top half of the chart) are self-contained. They keep their feelings private and are uncomfortable with physical contact. The most important thing for them is the task.

In general, relationship-oriented people (bottom half of the chart) are open. They are easy to get to know and like physical contact. You'll get a hug from them. The most important thing for them is the relationship.

If you're a get-the-job-done personality, you'll have trouble interacting with *other-oriented* people, who want to have everyone like them. They'll most likely see you as demanding and difficult. You'll most likely see them as too emotional and needy.

On the other side of the coin, it is usually a waste of time letting a get-the-job-done task-oriented type know how much you like them in order to build a relationship and have clear and meaningful communication. Get-the-job-done types just want to get things settled and move on to the next task. Approaching them on the level of getting it done will provide common ground, and they'll be more receptive to your ideas, believing that you are "their kind" of person.

Get-the-job-done personalities and get-the-job-done-*right* personalities often clash when one side wants speed and the other side wants perfection.

Get-the-job-done-*right* people don't want to get involved with the self-oriented people who are interested in being the center of attention. The get-the-job-done-*right* personalities are loners, not interested in following or in popularity contests.

The same thing applies in varying degrees to all types. Communicating at a level that the other person understands is a big step in dealing with the issues at hand.

Based on this, compare your profile to the difficult people in your workplace. Can you see what causes some of the behavioral issues you have with them? Are they more interested in getting the job done right while you're more interested in making sure everyone is satisfied with the work? Are they more interested in controlling the work while you're more interested in getting it done right? Are they standoffish, which you perceive as cold; are you friendly, which they perceive as gushy?

You can never be all things to all people, but with a little forethought and caring, you can approach people from a point of view they understand.

Too often, managers forget to use the most powerful communication tool of all. You can know all the tricks of communication, but your communication will never be as effective as when you layer it with prayer. Take time to breathe a prayer before speaking to someone. Ask God to facilitate your words and open the channels of understanding.

Three Truths about Difficult People

Regardless of how wonderful your job may be or how well you get along with your employees, no doubt there's still at least one difficult person you have to deal with. As a mindful manager, it is hard to admit that you don't get along with everyone, but the reality is that there'll always be people with whom you have relationship issues. Even Adam and Eve disagreed in the garden of Eden. How much more can you expect disagreement in the workday world of the twenty-first century?

There are three simple truths you need to know and believe before you begin to deal with the negative behavior of your difficult persons.

1. You're not the reason they are difficult.

As the manager, you may blame yourself for your difficult employees' negative behavior, thinking that something you are doing has caused it. This is especially true if an employee doesn't exhibit the same behavior with other managers or on other work teams. The truth is, a difficult employee may not act the same way with other managers or teams as he does with you. The bad news is that the employee has discovered that certain negative behaviors elicit a desired response from you. The difficult behavior pushes your buttons and causes a reaction.

2. You don't have to like a difficult employee to cope with the behavior.

Somewhere the idea has been propagated that we should like, even love, everyone. However, that love is only possible when it is a natural outgrowth of God's love for us. The harsh reality is that we're human, and although we can pray for our enemies and ask our higher power to help us overcome our dislike of certain people, we struggle just as much as anyone else with negative feelings. If you can get over having to like someone first before you deal with her behavior, you'll go a long way toward solving the problem. You may not like someone, but you can love with divine love—seeing each person as a child of God, just as you are.

3. You can't change difficult people.

How many relationships have ended because one person wanted to change another? It can't be done. Your difficult person isn't going to suddenly become a wonderful, caring, hardworking employee just because you want him to. You can't even change his negative behavior; only the difficult person can choose to change the behavior. What can you do? You can learn how to change your *reaction* to the negative behavior. This is a lot easier than you might think because God will support you. You can ask God to help you deal with your own behavior and then let go of worrying about how the other person behaves.

WHY PEOPLE BEHAVE AS THEY DO

Although there are a lot of underlying reasons for negative behavior in the workplace, that behavior is repeated for one simple reason: *what is rewarded is repeated.*

You may not be aware that you're actually rewarding your difficult employee's negative behavior. To you, it may seem that all you do is nag, cajole, threaten, warn, beg, or harass that employee to get the productivity level up. But there's a reward factor here that you may have overlooked.

Think about this scenario. A small child is in the supermarket with his mother. She's hurrying to complete her purchases. As they enter the store, she tells the child that if he's a good boy, she'll buy him a chocolate bar at the checkout counter. The child then tries to be good. However, as they come to the cereal aisle, he sees a cereal he likes. He starts to tell his mother about it. She is so intent on shopping, she ignores him. He speaks a bit louder, still trying to be good. Mother is now consulting her list and wheels past the cereals. In frustration, the little boy throws himself down on the floor and indulges in a full-blown tantrum. Now his mother notices him. So do half the people in the store. The little boy has learned a valuable lesson about behavior: *if you want attention, be bad!*

When this child gets to kindergarten, he's one of twenty-five students in the class. He starts out trying to be a good boy—raising his hand to ask permission, speaking quietly to his classmates, playing nicely on the playground. Then he paints a wonderful picture. He tries to get the teacher to notice it, but she's busy with the other twenty-four students. Finally, in frustration, he pours a pot of paint on the head of the little girl next to him. Now he has the teacher's attention. His early lesson is now confirmed: if you want attention, be bad!

He goes on to high school and college, maybe marries, gets a job, and begins his career. Still, that early lesson is a key to his behavior—if you want attention, be bad. This lesson is repeated over and over in life:

Who gets attention: the good child or the bad child?

Who gets attention: the good employee or the bad one?

Today, that grown-up boy works for you. He's your difficult person.

Human beings need to be noticed, to be counted, to be seen. In other words, they need attention. Difficult people exhibit negative behaviors because they've discovered those behaviors will garner them attention. Yes, it's negative attention, but it's still attention. Negative attention is better than no attention at all.

Think about a specific employee's negative behavior that you're dealing with right now. Jot down exactly what he or she does that you perceive as a problem. Then jot down how you react to that problem behavior.

THE REWARD FORMULA

Your reaction to the employee's negative behavior is the attention that your difficult person desires. Do you call the difficult person into your office to speak about the behavior? That's attention. Do you speak to the difficult person in anger and frustration? That's attention. Do you write up the incident in a performance appraisal? More attention. Do you speak to others concerning the negative behavior? Even more attention. Do you speak to the difficult person in front of other employees? Mega attention!

Yes, it's negative attention, but for that particular person, any attention is better than none at all.

Here's how the scenario plays out:

1. Your difficult person exhibits negative behavior.
2. You react to that negative behavior.
3. Your difficult person gets your attention.
4. Your reaction is the difficult person's reward for the negative behavior.
5. What is rewarded is repeated.

Because your difficult person enjoys the reward of your attention, she repeats the negative behavior anytime she feels neglected or ignored.

The secret to dealing with the negative behaviors of difficult people is to take away the reward. In other words, change your reaction to the behavior. Try to give it as little attention as possible in public. At the same time, you must begin to replace the attention for negative behavior by giving public attention to the employee when she is doing well, is productive, or is performing the job adequately. This may not be easy if you have a particularly difficult employee, but everyone does it right sometime. As the saying goes, try to catch that person doing right!

Now your difficult person will be rewarded for good behavior, and because attention is what the person craves, she will repeat the behavior.

THE SNAP TECHNIQUE

Wouldn't it be great to instantly have rapport with your employees, regardless of the baggage the relationship carries? Using the SNAP technique gives you the opportunity to provide that reward factor with your difficult people and also gives you the same opportunity to acknowledge those people on your team who are your best supporters on a regular basis.

STUDIES HAVE SHOWN THAT PEOPLE MAKE A DECISION ABOUT ANOTHER PERSON IN SEVEN SECONDS.

Studies have shown that people make a decision about another person in seven seconds. In that seven-second period, your employees will decide what kind of mood you are in, how you feel about them, and whether or not you care about them. SNAP involves only seven seconds, yet it is a powerful tool that if used regularly can make amazing changes to morale and well-being in your workplace.

To practice the SNAP technique when you see one of your employees, do the following:

S—Smile: Not a big teeth-baring, lip-stretching grin. Not a tight little grimace. Not an obviously phony smile that doesn't reach your eyes. Just relax your mouth and pull in the corners. This small movement changes your face dramatically and signals that you're relaxed, pleased to see this person, nonthreatening, not angry, emotionally present, and willing to engage with him or her.

N—Notice: Look the other person in the eyes. In the first moment or two of eye contact, a pulse of electricity flows between you and the other person. It's a powerful moment that bonds a relationship. If you're wondering how long to hold that eye contact, notice the color of the other person's eyes. By the time you've looked, noted the color, and looked away, you've held eye contact just long enough to avoid being seen as threatening or hostile.

A—Attend: Pay attention! The person is front of you is an open book if you'll take time to read the pages. How does he look? Happy, sad, anxious, worried, upset? Is he wearing something new, something that looks great on him? Does she have a new haircut? New glasses? How is he standing? Straight? Slumped?

P—Personal: Inject a personal touch in the interaction with a sentence or two. Try to gauge what is happening with him from that overall appearance scan and comment on it if you can. "That's a great tie!" or "Wow—you look busy today. Got a lot going on?" If you haven't deduced anything from your glance, then make an impersonal comment, but add a personal touch, such as, "Snowed a lot last night. Did you have trouble digging out your car?" This isn't the time to talk about work-related items. This is a time to connect with the other person on a human level. If the other person wants to engage in further conversation, he will. If not, the person will move on but will leave with a feeling that you took the time to acknowledge his presence.

There is no magic in getting along with employees. As a manager, you need to treat employees with respect and dignity—as you would want to be treated. Your job is to model the behavior and standards you expect of others. A mindful manager also knows the importance of providing nourishment for the heart. A manager who develops rapport with employees, treats them with respect, is aware of needs, and is fair and available is someone for whom employees will go the distance.

One of the paradoxes of workplace relationships is that they often are treated differently from relationships outside of the job. You may pray for your family, your friends, or even strangers you will never meet, yet you may not feel it appropriate to pray for your employees. What would happen if you decided to pray for those who work with you?

Each day on your way to work or in a moment of quiet time, think of one employee. Ask God to be present in your relationship with this employee, to show you the needs of the employee, and to use you to care for that employee.

Praying for your employees is not always easy. For some people, you'll need to get past any prejudices, dislikes, or anger that may exist in the relationship. Begin by acknowledging your negative feelings to God. Ask forgiveness for your failures in the relationship. Accept that forgiveness and move on to your desires for the well-being of the person. End by thanking God for caring.

As you begin this prayer adventure, you can expect changes and small miracles in your workplace. You'll find that God does give you knowledge and insight into how to communicate effectively with your team. Through the discernment that comes with God-centered prayer, you'll be able to empower, nurture, and build up the people who have been placed in your care.

8

LEARNING TO HEAR
BEYOND WORDS

Great communicators say that listening is the first and greatest skill, and all the rest—speaking, persuading, and teaching—come after. Listening is an art and a skill, and like other skills, it requires discipline. As a manager, listening is your most important communication skill with your employees, far more valuable than talking or telling. Listening is a primary skill when you counsel, manage, and solve problems.

The New Testament story of the sower and the seed illustrates the significance of hearing and understanding what is being said. Some words fall by the wayside when the hearer doesn't understand them, and they are lost. Some words fall on rocky ground where they have no roots, and their message lasts only a short time. Some words fall among the thorns, where they are blocked off by outside influences. However, when the hearer is truly listening, the words fall on fertile ground and yield results.

That's why you need to understand what's involved in listening and then develop the necessary techniques to be silent and listen. You'll need to ignore your own thoughts and biases and concentrate attention on the person speaking. Hearing becomes listening only when you pay attention to what is said.

A manager who can listen effectively will be more likely to understand the problem and convey to the other person an attitude that "I care how you feel and think, and I'll help you without taking over." The employee becomes more willing to open up and examine the problem in a new light.

Unfortunately, listening is a poorly developed skill in most managers. Managers are more likely to talk and tell instead of listen and learn. You may think you are listening, but in reality you're not paying close attention. For example, when you listen to the radio in the morning as you are getting ready to come to work, you tune in those items that interest you and tune out those that don't. You use that same habit in casual conversations, and all too often in conversations you have in the workplace. You may find yourself mindlessly saying, "Uh-huh," only then to have to say, "I'm sorry, what did you say?" Instead of listening, you are busy formulating your own response to the speaker.

Bad listening habits on the part of a manager can leave those not listened to feeling frustrated, angry, hurt, and resentful—feelings unlikely to enhance productivity.

Rate Your Listening Skills

Directions: For each question, give yourself a number score, based on your typical work conversations.

   1 = Never
   2 = Seldom
   3 = Sometimes
   4 = Usually
   5 = Always

_____ 1. Do you find yourself understanding what was said but not what was meant?

_____ 2. Do you have trouble concentrating on what the person is saying because of external distractions such as noise or movement?

_____ 3. Do you have trouble concentrating on what the person is saying because of internal distractions such as worry, fear, or daydreaming?

_____ 4. Do you find yourself responding to what the speaker implies, rather than what he or she really says?

_____ 5. Do you respond with anger to words, stated or implied, that for all logical reasons should not make you angry?

_____ 6. Do you have trouble reading a person's body language?

_____ 7. Do you find it hard to respond nonjudgmentally to a speaker if you disagree with him or her?

_____ 8. Do you find it hard to respond nonjudgmentally to a speaker if you dislike him or her?

_____ 9. Do you mentally prepare your response before the speaker has finished?

_____ 10. Do you find yourself listening selectively, hearing only those words or ideas that you want to hear?

_____ 11. Do certain words, phrases, or actions consistently trigger either negative or positive responses in you?

_____ 12. Do you find yourself asking, "What did you say?" even though you've been listening to the speaker?

_____ 13. Do you rely on others to interpret what was said at a meeting?

Add up your score for all the questions: _____

If you scored:

- 13–20: Congratulations! You're a very good listener.
- 21–32: You're a fairly good listener.
- 33–45: You're an average listener.
- 46–58: You're a fairly poor listener.
- 59–65: Your listening skills could use some sharpening!

THE FOUR KEY AREAS OF MASTER LISTENERS

Have you ever enjoyed talking to a master listener? You just know that the person is *really* listening to you, aware of meanings beyond your words and interested in the full context of your message. You don't know why you feel that way—you just know that you feel safe and secure in talking to this person. You can become a master listener too by using the same listening techniques that give a master listener's assurance to people who talk to you.

Empathetic Listening

Empathetic listeners encourage people to talk, articulate feelings, and express themselves openly. They are careful to tune in to the feelings behind the words. In a work crisis, a manager with empathetic listening skills may have an employee who says, "No, there's nothing wrong." The manager can read beyond the words and understand that the employee is feeling insecure and stressed over the situation but doesn't want to appear incompetent. The manager can then gently elicit the employee's true feelings about the situation.

Analytical Listening

Analytical listeners are adept at separating fact from fantasy, enthusiasm from evidence. They can recognize major ideas and separate them from minor ones. They don't get sidetracked by details, digressions, or repetitions. In a confrontational situation, angry workers will often bring in side stories and old history to obfuscate the real issue. An analytical listener can sift through the chaff of unrelated information and find the kernel of truth within it.

Integrative Listening
Integrative listeners are able to utilize others' ideas by adapting and adopting them. They assume that people wish to contribute, so they encourage the more reticent people to speak up. In a departmental meeting, the integrative listener continually elicits responses from those who have not yet contributed to the discussion.

Holistic Listening
Holistic listeners understand that messages are presented through personal filters and biases. They also understand that their own messages will be perceived in the same way. For example, if an employee is a constant complainer, the manager will hear all the messages from that employee through a personal filter that expects all information to be a complaint. If the manager has a habit of ignoring the complaint, then the employee probably won't hear any helpful words in the manager's response. In the same way, someone with an age bias may give less credence to a message from an older person than one from a younger person. Similarly, the older person may ignore information if it is presented by a younger person.

How to Be an Active Listener
There is a distinction between merely *hearing another's words* and *really listening for her message*. Active listening enables you to understand what the person is thinking or feeling. It is as if you are standing in the other

person's shoes—seeing through her eyes and listening through her ears. Your own viewpoint may differ, and you may not necessarily agree with the person, but as you listen, you begin to understand her perspective.

It's hard to really listen to a difficult employee. If you're struggling with your feelings toward that person—trying to overcome animosity or dislike, feeling guilty that your faith doesn't seem to overcome your feelings—listening to the person will be a challenge and a chore.

Fortunately you can develop better listening habits if you take the time to learn and practice them. Because you think three times faster than you talk, you can use that interim time to help you respond better to the speaker. Above all, your attitude will govern how well you listen. If you genuinely want to help the speaker and are willing to put aside your needs and intentions, then you will be a better listener.

When an employee starts to speak to you, get in the habit of asking for help to really hear him. A simple prayer such as, "God, open my ears, open my mind, and open my heart to this person," is all you need to do.

Then start to listen by lining up your nonverbal messages to the person. Your nonverbal behavior will tell the speaker at once if you are tuned in to the conversation and involved in it. If you look at your watch at the start of the conversation, you are sending the message that you are busy and don't have time for the conversation. If you fold your arms across your chest, you are signaling your unwillingness to listen and receive information from the person. An open, relaxed posture, fully facing the speaker, says that you're ready to be engaged with him. Lean slightly toward the other person if you are sitting; smile and nod your head where appropriate. Crossed arms and legs are closed positions, so avoid them. Also, don't fidget or play with pens or pencils.

Making eye contact (but not staring) communicates you are interested in the speaker's words. Practice in a mirror by maintaining eye contact with yourself while telling a story about your vacation or hobby. Notice your eyes and face. Do you seem relaxed?

Next, tell yourself about a problem at work. Compared to your response to pleasant stories, do your eyes and face change as you speak about problems?

Practicing this technique allows you to express openness and acceptance as you listen to a speaker.

The location you select to meet with an employee communicates mindfulness too. A noisy, crowded lunchroom is not a good place to talk about serious matters, so move to a quieter place. If you can't do that, let the speaker know you want to hear what she has to say, and set a time for the discussion as soon as possible. If the conversation is in your office, come out from behind your desk and have phone calls held.

Don't interrupt the speaker until the message is delivered, but do make appropriate sounds to encourage him. These sounds show someone you are following what he is saying. Sounds like "ah," or "ummm," or "oh," when used appropriately, show the speaker his message is getting through. Be careful not to overuse these sounds, as they can become annoying and distracting. You can also encourage the speaker by using actual words. You might say, "I see" or "Really?" As with the sounds, don't overdo these comments.

Asking questions at the appropriate time encourages the speaker to continue and also shows you're listening. You might say something like, "You felt your efforts were being ignored, then?" Questions can also deal with the content of the message, as in, "What happened when the parts finally arrived?" Don't break in on the speaker's words to ask a question. Be careful not to interrupt. Only ask a question when you assess the speaker has finished with a thought.

REFLECTING BACK THE MESSAGE

Once the message has been delivered, it's your job to let the other person know that you heard him or her. This is done by using reflecting skills. The speaker will be frustrated if you didn't listen well enough to know what the message was.

1. Paraphrase

When you paraphrase, you are saying, "This is what I heard you say. This is how I interpreted your message." The speaker can then let you know if you are correct, or let you know how you missed what she said. For example, you might paraphrase a long explanation of a problem by saying, "Do I have it right—you felt you had no option under the circumstances but to shut the machines down?" This is where your extra mental speed over the speaker's verbal speed allows you to sort out what she is saying and organize your paraphrase.

2. Reflect Emotions

Here you use questions to reflect to the speaker that you acknowledge his emotions. Emotions are detected in the tone and facial expressions of the speaker. Fear, happiness, disappointment, and anger can all be detected if you listen reflectively. Listen for emotional or "hot" words such as *sexist* and *stupid*, but be careful that you don't get hooked emotionally by these words so you no longer listen effectively. Try not to read emotion from the speaker just because you think you'd be emotional about the problem, when, in fact, the speaker may not be emotional at all. You might hear a sharp retort, "I'm *not* angry." But if you do detect anger in the speaker, you might respond, "It sounds like you were angered by my review of your work."

By showing you want to understand the problem and its emotional impact on the speaker, you make the speaker feel better understood.

When you use reflective listening, you gain a better understanding of what the speaker is saying. By encouraging the speaker to talk at greater depth, you may expose hidden problems. The relationship between you and the speaker will improve as you develop greater openness and trust.

Reflective listening can create motivational energy. Because you showed you were accepting and encouraging but didn't try to diagnose and solve the problem for the speaker, the speaker is more likely to recognize and put into practice new ways to act.

WHY YOU HAVE TROUBLE LISTENING TO SOMEONE

Some communication barriers make it difficult to listen. Barriers to communication are obstacles that distort or block the flow of needed information. Suppose someone said to you, "The number 5 machine is broken." It seems a simple, clear message, so how could your feedback be less than perfect?

You may have a tendency to judge or evaluate the sender and the message as good or bad. Perhaps the sender is an employee with whom you've had trouble in the past. You might think or even say, "I'll bet he did something stupid." Even if you don't respond that directly, he'll sense you blaming him for the problem and will become defensive, which will make it harder to understand the problem and deal with it.

You and the sender may have different perceptions of the message. *Broken* to the speaker may mean the machine won't start; to you it may imply a machine part has failed. You can easily imagine the following flow of messages:

"Which part has failed?"

"No part has failed."

"I thought you said it was broken!"

"That's right."

Instead ask a simple question that checks your perception:

"What do you mean by *broken?*"

You and the sender may have different intentions. You might automatically read into the sender's message an intention on his part that isn't there. For example, you might decide he is pleased to be the bearer of bad news that will cause you problems, when that was never his intention. Instead of taking the news calmly and getting on with the problem, you might reply, "I'll bet you're pleased about this," which puts the employee on the defensive and makes the problem harder to deal with.

You may ignore nonverbal signals. Your employee might well be nervous about being the bearer of bad news and show it by avoiding eye contact with you or by tapping his foot. You have to deal with the emotion, or you run the danger of making him less sure of himself by ignoring it. "How do you know?" can sound very different if he is nervous. Don't forget, the barriers work in both directions, so his reply to you also can be affected.

As you listen to others, trust that God will help you tune in to what they are really saying. Be still; allow your heart as well as your mind to open up to the person who is speaking. Pray for guidance and understanding. Say little—your attitude will be all the other person needs to feel that her words are being heard, understood, and received. Be mindful of God with you, acting as an intermediary between you and the employee.

9

RELYING ON
THE POWER OF GOD

Regardless of the kind of management position you may have, there is an inherent power that comes with being the boss. At some level, you have the authority to oversee the work of others, assign projects, evaluate productivity, and deal with personnel issues. Your power may be limited or limitless, but either way, you have an edge over those who work for you. As a mindful manager, you realize that how you use that power says a lot about the kind of manager you are and your attitude toward the people who work with you.

Different kinds of power are available to a manager.

Legitimate power: This power comes from the position you have in the organization that grants you the right to have authority over others.

Reward power: This power is the ability you have as a manager to reward those who work for you. You can provide something your employees want and so influence them to act in a certain way. Obvious rewards are pay raises and promotions. If you don't have the legitimate power to offer these, you can also give less tangible rewards, such as praise, recognition, and acceptance.

Coercive power: This power, the opposite of reward power, allows you to control others with punishments, such as demotions and suspension, or to take away rewards in a job, such as generous benefits. Few managers today have the coercive power that once went with the position in more hierarchical work settings.

Referent power: Have you ever really admired another manager? Did that person have charisma? Charismatic leaders have influence because others admire them and want to be like them. Was there a manager in your work experience whom you were more anxious to please than other managers? If so, that person had referent power. Referent power is the most effective way to lead others. Moses, who led the Israelites out of Egypt and onto the Promised Land, exhibited referent power. In the same way, Jesus had referent power too. People followed him, not because of an exalted position, not because of wealth and standing, but because he had personal traits that drew others to him.

Expert power: People with expert skills are also powerful. Because a computer salesperson has expert knowledge about computers, she can persuade you to buy her company's computer system. Clearly, to be a manager of a computer information systems group, you would need to have the authority that computer expertise brings in addition to the legitimate power you would have as a manager. But expert power need not be aligned with other forms of power. An administrative assistant who has little legitimate power, but who is the only one who understands a complex filing system, has expert power.

Information power: This form of power is similar to expert power—it is the ability to share or withhold information and to control its accuracy. An administrative assistant may possess considerable power in the organization because he can control the information that others receive.

Your power as a mindful manager comes from God. If you are mindful of God's presence, then the power to manage effectively is available to you. However, God has also given you the ability to speak, to assert yourself, and to persuade others. By understanding how human beings interact with others and using your knowledge of communication, you can be assured that your message is clearly heard and understood.

THE THREE VS OF COMMUNICATION

All communication is made up of three aspects:

Verbal: the words that you speak.

Vocal: the voice and tone you use.

Visual: your body language.

You may think that words are the most important aspect of communication. You may spend time on getting the words right—running through a script in your head, thinking about what you want to say, choosing the correct words to impart meaning to your conversation. However, only 7 percent of the communication between two individuals comes from the words they speak![1]

Your voice, on the other hand, imparts more information than your words do. Nearly 40 percent of what you have to say comes from your voice—the volume, rate, pitch, and tone quality that you use. The meaning of words can be altered significantly by changing the intonation of your voice. Consider the words *I love you.* If you say them with warmth and feeling, the listener gets the message. But what if you say them with sarcasm? The meaning changes dramatically, although the words remain the same.

Your words and the tone of your voice make up less than half of the meaning you want to convey to the other person. That leaves over half of your message to be communicated through body language alone. The way you stand, your facial expressions, your hand gestures, your mannerisms—all have enormous impact on your message.

Some studies suggest over 90 percent of the meaning we derive from communication comes from the nonverbal cues that the other person gives. Often a person says one thing but communicates something totally different through vocal intonation and body language. These mixed signals force the receiver to choose between the verbal and nonverbal parts of the message. Most often, the receiver chooses the nonverbal aspects. Mixed messages create tension and distrust because the receiver senses that the communicator is hiding something or is being less than candid.

You can reinforce your message with nonverbal signals. If you are making a joke, your posture will be relaxed, your mouth smiling, and your head nodding. If you're conveying bad news, your voice will be low and somber, your body still, and your face neutral or sympathetic.

If you don't really believe what you are saying, your nonverbal messages can give away your true feelings. Avoiding eye contact, shuffling your feet, or folding your arms across the front of your body—all express far more than the words you're speaking.

Nonverbal messages can substitute for a verbal message. For example, your eyes can convey a far more vivid message than words. Also, nonverbal messages complement the words. A manager who pats a person on the back in addition to giving praise can increase the impact of the message. Nonverbal communication can underline a verbal message as well. Pounding the table will certainly emphasize an angry message.

Skillful communicators understand the importance of nonverbal communication and use it to increase their effectiveness, as well as interpret it to understand more clearly what someone else is really saying.

Because such a large portion of your messages comes from nonverbal communication, it is important to know what makes up the nonverbal part of your messages.

Nonverbal Messages You Send

Body language. This includes facial movements, such as glances, frowns, yawns, sighs; finger taps; doodling; eye contact, such as staring or glaring; various arm and leg movements; touching one's hair, knees, forehead, or chin; head scratching or beard stroking; posture; stride or pace when walking; blushing; and perspiring. Of course we can easily misread these cues, especially when communicating across cultures where gestures can mean something very different. For example, in North American culture, a person signals agreement by nodding the head up and down, whereas in India, a person moves his or her head from side to side to indicate agreement.

We also look to posture and gestures for clues about the communicator. The way we stand and the way we hold our hands can indicate self-confidence, aggressiveness, fear, guilt, or anxiety.

Touching. This involves touching the other person to impart meaning, as in a handshake, a pat on the back, an arm around the shoulder, a kiss, or a hug. Our culture sets limits on acceptable touching behavior. Status, age, and gender are factors. Notice how often a politician reaches out to grasp the arm of the hand he is shaking, or how often she puts an arm around another's shoulders. It is the politician's way of connecting with voters beyond words, gestures, and posture.

The relationship of time to communication. When meetings start and end, the frequency and nature of staff meetings, the amount of time allotted to interpersonal interaction, valuing another person's time—all indicate how you view others. Think how a subordinate and a boss view arriving for an agreed-upon meeting. The boss might not worry about being late; the employee would strive to be punctual.

Use of space around you to define your territory. Most people are uncomfortable when someone stands very close to them. They feel their space has been invaded. People extend their territory to attain power and intimacy. They can define their territory either with permanent walls or with possessions, such as a notebook, coat, or pen. For Americans, the intimate zone is about two feet around a person. This varies in other cultures. The personal zone, from about two to four feet, usually is reserved for family and friends. Within the social zone of four to twelve feet most business transactions take place. The public zone, usually over twelve feet, is used for formal presentations.[2]

Rhythmical communication between senders and receivers. This is when both parties begin to use the same body movements and speech patterns. Sometimes called mirroring, this powerful communication tool gives the receiver a sense of connection with the sender.

When you understand how the dynamics of communication—your words, your voice, and your body language—interact, you can then begin to use your power in an effective way.

THE POWER OF ASSERTIVENESS

What is assertiveness? It is getting your thoughts across in a straightforward manner without harming others. This doesn't mean that you can disguise aggressive behavior as assertiveness. In any situation where your words or actions cause the other person to feel intimidated, powerless, uncomfortable, or threatened, you're being aggressive, not assertive.

Assertiveness is more than something you do; assertiveness is who you are. How you view yourself will shape your behavior both positively and negatively. Becoming assertive begins within your mind. If you are not comfortable with yourself, then assertiveness is just another manipulative game. The bottom line is that assertive people like themselves.

Believing that you are a loved child of God, that you are worthy of divine love, and that you can be a conduit of that love to others is the foundation for assertiveness.

What Is Your Self-Awareness?

Directions: Read the following words and underline every word that describes you.

Accepting	Impulsive	Quiet	Adaptive
Innovative	Realistic	Belligerent	Joyful
Reflective	Bold	Judgmental	Rigid
Careless	Kind	Sarcastic	Clever
Knowledgeable	Serious	Dependable	Loving
Sociable	Domineering	Logical	Tactful
Tense	Trusting	Uncertain	Warm
Wishful	Withdrawn	Witty	Worried
Curious	Sad	Confident	Effective
Energetic	Fearful	Foolish	Free
Friendly	Gruff	Guilty	Happy
Perceptive	Quarrelsome	Passive	Organized
Objective	Modest	Manipulative	Noisy
Anxious	Humorous	Excitable	Shy
Demanding	Smart	Slow	Pushy
Loud	Stressed	Worn out	

You just labeled yourself! The words you chose define your self-image. What do your word choices reveal about your assertiveness? What do they say about your relationship with God? Are the words you picked different from words your parents or friends would use to describe you?

An assertive adult can make an honest list of her own strengths and weaknesses without denying either list.

How do you know when you're being assertive?

1. Assertive responses are characterized by the use of "I" statements instead of "You" statements. For example: "I am disappointed when you cannot complete your assignment on time," instead of, "You never get your work done on time, and that disappoints me."
2. Assertive responses are usually effective in getting others to change or reinforce behavior.
3. Assertive responses run a low risk of hurting a relationship.
4. Assertive responses neither attack others nor put them on the defensive.
5. Assertive behavior prevents "gunnysacking," that is, saving up a lot of bad feelings. Some people find it hard to express their feelings, so they bite their tongues and say nothing. Finally something happens—the proverbial straw that breaks the camel's back—and they explode. In doing so, they bring up all those other instances when their feelings were hurt. In some cases, the feelings go back years in the relationship.

WHAT IS YOUR ASSERTIVENESS STYLE?

Directions: Mark each of the following statements Y (yes) or N (no).

_____ 1. When making a point, I often point my finger at people.
_____ 2. I stare at people I don't like.
_____ 3. I have been known to yell or shout when I'm angry.
_____ 4. When walking with someone, I'm usually one step ahead.
_____ 5. I can't stand to wait in line.

_____ 6. I am good at verbal put-downs.

_____ 7. I often interrupt others.

_____ 8. I get the conversation rolling in a group.

_____ 9. I don't forget—and I do get even.

_____ 10. People have told me they are afraid of me.

_____ 11. I often talk with my hand over my mouth.

_____ 12. I often reply with, "Nothing, I'm just thinking."

_____ 13. I'm uncomfortable making eye contact with people I hardly know.

_____ 14. I tend to slump when sitting.

_____ 15. I don't like to whine or complain.

_____ 16. I usually ask permission to be excused if I need to leave a staff meeting.

_____ 17. When I'm angry, I smile to hide it.

_____ 18. I apologize for the weather.

_____ 19. I don't like arguments.

_____ 20. People take advantage of me.

_____ 21. I can say no without feeling guilty.

_____ 22. I have a reputation for being a good listener.

_____ 23. I'm willing to step out and say what I think.

_____ 24. I seldom lose control of my emotions.

_____ 25. I don't get nervous at my performance reviews.

_____ 26. I don't mind making mistakes—I learn from them.

_____ 27. I like to try new restaurants.

_____ 28. I fall asleep easily.

_____ 29. I am content with my life.

_____ 30. I share information, thoughts, and feelings with the members of my team.

Now add the number of yes answers for questions 1–10: ___. Yes responses in this section indicate *aggressive tendencies*. Aggressive responses may signal that you are a strong leader. You probably feel that you are stronger, more able, in some ways better than other people. However, others probably see you in a more negative light. You may not care about winning any popularity contests and you may get a lot done, but you're also in danger of making enemies and causing resentment. When you engage in aggressive communication, you:

- Leave others feeling put down by you.
- Choose for others rather than allowing others to choose for themselves.
- Come across as hostile and defensive.
- Rely on sarcasm, name-calling, threats, blaming, insults.

Next, add the number of yes answers for questions 11–20: ___. Yes responses here indicate *passive tendencies*. You are a nice person, but you could be telling others that they can treat you badly. Your communication may be saying that they are stronger, more able, or even better than you believe yourself to be. When practicing passive behavior, you:

- Deny your own feelings and opinions.
- Allow others to choose for you.
- Feel guilty and angry.

Finally, add the number of yes answers for questions 21–30: ___. Yes responses in this section indicate *assertive tendencies*. Assertiveness leads to win/win solutions and a tendency to feel good about yourself and others. When you practice assertive behavior, you:

- Openly, directly express your thoughts and feelings.
- Allow others to choose for themselves.

- Seek mutual satisfaction at achieving a desired goal.

In addition to aggressive, passive, and assertive behaviors, there is a fourth behavior: passive-aggressive. People who are passive-aggressive give mixed messages. Their words, body language, and tone of voice do not match. They may sound passive, but their body language is aggressive. Or they may sound aggressive, but they don't back it up with tone or nonvisual messages. Most passive-aggressive people aren't aware that they're using this mode of communication. The passive-aggressive person might be that employee in the meeting who sits silently, arms folded across his chest, a sour look on his face—yet when you ask him what's wrong, he'll reply, "Oh, nothing important." His body language is aggressive; his words are passive.

Finally, **look at your totals for all the different sections.** Which one has the greatest number of yes answers? The highest number indicates your communication preference: aggressive, passive, or assertive. Does the result surprise you? If you have two totals very close to each other, it usually means that you use both styles, switching from one to the other as the situation warrants. For example, you may start out aggressively in an interaction, but if the other person also becomes aggressive, you may back off to a passive stance.

In a nutshell, assertiveness is all about rights. An aggressive person believes that she has the right to express an opinion and be heard, but the other party doesn't. The passive person believes that the other party has the right to express an opinion and be heard, but he doesn't. The passive-aggressive person gives mixed messages: no one is sure of his or her rights when dealing with such a person. The assertive person believes that both sides in a communication have the right to express an opinion and the right to be heard.

ASSERTIVENESS STRATEGIES FOR MANAGERS

1. Learn to Say No

This may seem to be a simple matter, but it is a vital skill. Avoid saying "Maybe," "I really need to think about it," or "I'm pretty busy right now." Instead practice saying no when you don't want to do something. It is easy once you learn how.

Listen attentively to the request. Ask questions so you can decide if it is something you wish to do or not. Consider the request for a few seconds. Pray. Listen to the voice within you—your gut reaction. Don't fret about being right or wrong. Your prayer has been heard, and you can rely on God to answer. Know that on some occasions you might want to say no, but the inner voice is telling you to say yes. Or the opposite might be true. When feeling conflicted about a request, remember to pray, pause, reflect, and respond.

Give reasons for saying no. In most instances, you will have a valid reason. You may say something like, "I can't change the vacation schedule for our team at this late date. Many people have already made vacation plans." If you respond in the way that you think God wants you to, yet you're not sure of the reasons behind your response, be assertive and say so: "I feel I need to say no right now. Can I think about this and get back to you?" Don't be pressured into making excuses. You have the right to take time to think through something. In the same way, be prepared to give others the same consideration if you ask them to do something and they say no.

Suggest options and when possible allow others to work out a solution: "I suggest that you speak to the others, and if someone is willing to switch vacation days with you, I'm willing to make the change." If no viable options present themselves, again ask for time to reflect on the situation, or ask the other person for input and suggestions.

2. Address the Problem, not the Person

When you're faced with the need to confront someone on your staff, use the EASY process for addressing the problem, not the personality. The EASY process ensures that you are assertive, that you make your concerns clear, and that you give the other person an opportunity to respond. What is the EASY process?

E—Express. Start with an "I" statement rather than a "You" statement. Instead of saying, "You don't care about our staff meetings," say, "I feel that you're not taking our staff meetings seriously." Many managers are uncomfortable using "I" language and try to avoid taking a personal stance. They say, "The company expects . . ." "The policy is . . ." There is enormous power in using the word *I*. It tells the other person that you are personally engaged, that you are taking responsibility for the confrontation, and that you are willing to deal with the issue at hand.

A—Address. Address the problem by stating it clearly. Stick to the facts and avoid broad generalizations, such as, "You're always either late for our staff meetings or skip them altogether. No wonder you don't know what's going on." Broad generalizations are easy to make, but they carry the baggage of a personal attack; in many cases, they give the other person an opportunity to counterattack on a personal level. "I was at the meeting last month, and if you think I'm not up to speed on my assignment, it's because you don't give me all the information."

Instead you could say, "The meeting minutes show that you have been late for the last four meetings and missed two meetings before that. Not being at those meetings means you've missed some vital information you need to complete your assignment."

S—Suggest. Now it is time to suggest a solution to the problem. Have a solution ready before you begin the EASY process. You could say something like, "Here's what we're going to do. I'll make sure that another staff person reminds you when we have a meeting so you'll be able to attend." Or, "It seems reasonable to ask you to be at all staff meetings since they are part of your job expectations."

Y—*Yes.* At this point, it is vital to get agreement from the other person. This is an opportunity for the other person to express, explain, or excuse. Say, "Can you agree to that solution?"

Since you have the legitimate power to expect agreement, you may indicate any consequences that would result from noncompliance. However, when you are working from the base of referent power—power that comes from your personal impact on others—the other person should feel a desire to solve the problem with you.

Keep in mind that the words you are using convey less than 10 percent of the message. You'll want to be aware of the tone of your voice, which should be reasonable and nonaccusatory, and of your body language, which should be relaxed and open.

3. Make Good Decisions and Don't Vacillate

Making good decisions can be difficult. Uncertainty, changing your mind after coming to a decision, getting cold feet, being afraid of the risks—all may make it difficult for you to come to a decision. However, nothing labels you as passive so quickly as the inability to make a decision and stick to it. If you have trouble sticking with a decision, break down the steps that follow up on that decision. After you've made the decision, what will you need to do first? Second? Next? Don't look at anything except the immediate step you are presently taking. Don't look at the next step until you have completed the one you are on. Don't look at the big picture until you get to the end of your single steps.

Trust God to help you make a good decision. Many managers fail to pray about their daily work, feeling that it is beneath God's interest, less important than praying for the sick, or a waste of God's time. Make a habit of offering each decision of your day to God.

4. Know Your Limitations

Understand the structure, culture, and political mores of your company. You cannot always handle every problem, even if you are naturally assertive. Some things have to be taken to another level of authority. The biblical prophets often spoke of God as the final authority to turn to. Know what you can handle and then do that. Use the power you have sparingly. Managers who crack down continually, unfairly, or too strictly hamper their workers and end up lowering morale and production.

The mindful manager has another option not available to others—the authority of God as the final source of power. Ask for divine help when you are feeling uncomfortable about exerting your authority.

ASSERTIVENESS TOOLS

To practice assertiveness, keep in mind the following techniques.

Keep It Short

To keep yourself from becoming enmeshed in your own words, respond in short sentences. Don't overexplain or overelaborate.

Slow Down

When you feel challenged, your rate of speech accelerates. Discipline yourself to slow down. When you speak slowly, your thoughts sound more logical.

Deepen Your Voice

Stress can tighten your vocal cords, making your voice sound higher than normal. This higher pitch sends a signal that you are vulnerable. If you feel your throat tighten, slow your speech and make a determined effort to relax the muscles in your neck and shoulders.

Use a Firm Tone
To determine how tone works, say aloud the following sentence several times, using what you consider to be a passive, aggressive, and then assertive voice: "I need a staff member to work overtime on Friday."

Paraphrase
Summarize what the other person has said. You communicate two things when you paraphrase—I'm listening, and I'm paying attention.

Stick to the Facts
Instead of saying, "You're rude," state the facts: "You just interrupted me." Give other people the benefit of the doubt. If you're not sure what they are saying, ask them to rephrase or repeat their words.

Keep Habitual Behaviors in Check
Keep an eye on some of your habitual behaviors: don't interrupt, don't answer for other people, don't lose eye contact, don't write notes while someone is speaking, don't stop to answer the phone during the discussion, don't go silent, don't label people or ideas, and don't play psychologist.

THE KEY TO POWER: PERSUASION, NOT AUTHORITY
Even when you have legitimate or reward power over others, there are limits to its effectiveness. You may have the legitimate power to tell your staff to do something, but persuading them instead of requiring them will ensure they are more likely to carry out the task with enthusiasm and commitment. Persuasion involves others taking over your desire and owning it themselves, so they are now doing something because they

want to. In other words, persuasion can motivate an employee far more than the use of power.

Here are three strategies for motivating others through persuasion.

1. Establish Your Credibility

People are influenced by those they like, are attracted to, and respect. These attributes can be summed up as credibility. Advertisers use likable famous people to endorse their products. Because you like them and think they are competent and have integrity, you are persuaded to buy the product they endorse. Having credibility means others see you as competent, trustworthy, dependable, and honest. You have to earn the respect of others and continue earning it.

Your credibility will enhance your ability to persuade employees. But you have to be consistent. Show yourself to be undependable or dishonest, and you will have to rebuild your credibility from scratch.

Despite your best efforts, you may find that not everyone sees you as credible. You may have had to discipline someone who now regards you as an enemy. Be prepared for rejection now and then. Even Jesus had trouble establishing credibility in his hometown, where townsfolk saw him only as the son of Joseph the carpenter.

2. Use Evidence

When you are trying to persuade someone to a course of action, you will need to give them a reason to act in the way you want. "Why should I?" they might ask. To answer that question, you need to prepare evidence ahead of time. People will more easily buy into your arguments if they are based on logic and fact.

Try to put yourself in the other's shoes. What kind of argument will best persuade this person? What kinds of negative responses will she give to a particular argument? Given those responses, what arguments can you use in turn to support your proposal? Facts are most convincing at countering negative responses. The employee might say, "I like the old way we handled the invoices. I can do them more quickly that way." You can reply, "Yes, it will take some time to learn the new system, but with it, the same work is done in half the time, which will leave you more time for your customer calls."

People are persuaded if they can see how your arguments support their needs and goals. So be aware of the world's most-listened-to radio station: WII-FM—What's-In-It-For-Me? In most interactions, that is the underlying question, and if you can answer that question, you'll find others are more easily persuaded. In the example above, the manager was aware that the employee, a sales representative, made most of his money from customer calls. Spending a lot of time processing invoices took away available time to make those calls. What was in the new invoicing system for the employee was time to make more money.

Before you approach people with the intention of persuading them to adopt your idea or suggestion, determine their WII-FM.

3. Remember God Is with You

The mindful manager allows God to be part of all the interactions of the day. By tapping into the power that comes from God and flows through you, you exude an underlying confidence that makes your communication with employees compelling and effective.

Learning the techniques of good communication and employing them daily is helpful, but God's presence in you will add power to your words, tone, and body language.

10

TURNING WORKPLACE CONFLICT INTO BLESSING

Do you believe that all conflict is bad? Do you feel uncomfortable and ill at ease when it occurs? At work, do you try to avoid conflict or even ignore it when you can? If so, you're not alone. Most people want to avoid conflict.

Yet from the moment God created human beings and gave them free will, conflict became a reality in interpersonal relationships. Adam and Eve hadn't spent long in the Garden before they were engaged in conflict over eating the forbidden fruit. The Christian church through the ages has been divided by conflict and schisms. Most religions from Islam to Judaism suffer from splinter groups and dissenting sects. On a larger scale, the world has been torn apart by conflict, culminating in two world wars, ongoing battles, and skirmishes and fighting in our present time.

If you're like most managers, no one told you that you would have to be a peacekeeper, referee, and mediator for squabbling employees. Yet that is what happens in many workplaces.

Given this background, no wonder most people see conflict as a bad thing. However, conflict in the workplace can encourage positive change and growth, and depending on the way you deal with it, can allow new ideas to surface that otherwise might never be expressed.

There are different styles of dealing with conflict: you may be a controller, accommodator, collaborator, appeaser, or avoider. Understanding your approach to conflict will help you elicit the best outcome from all parties.

What Is Your Conflict Resolution Style?

Directions: For each statement, circle all of the responses that express the way you respond to conflict. You don't have to limit yourself to one response per question. Circle as many as apply to you.

1. When you have strong feelings in a conflict situation, you:
   A. Enjoy the emotional release and sense of exhilaration.
   B. Relish the challenge of the conflict.
   C. Become concerned about how others are feeling and thinking.
   D. Fear that someone might get hurt.
   E. Become convinced there is nothing you can do to resolve the situation.

2. You expect conflict to result in:
   A. Helping people face facts.
   B. Canceling out extremes in thinking so a middle ground can be reached.
   C. Clearing the air, enhancing commitment and results.
   D. Drawing people closer together.
   E. Assigning blame where it belongs.

3. When you have the authority in a conflict situation, you:
   A. Attempt to be direct and let others know your point of view.
   B. Try to negotiate the best settlement.
   C. Ask for other viewpoints and look for agreement.
   D. Go along with the others, providing support if they need it.
   E. Stick to the rules, the facts, and the regulations—by the book.

4. When someone takes an unreasonable position, you:
   A. Lay it on the line and tell them you don't like it.
   B. Are subtle in your approach—you may use humor to avoid confrontation.
   C. Show where you disagree and look for mutually acceptable solutions.
   D. Say nothing to the other person.
   E. Show with silence or facial expressions how you feel.

5. When you're angry with a coworker, you:
   A. Explode without giving it too much thought.
   B. Smooth things over by joking.
   C. Express your anger and ask them how the coworker feels.
   D. Pretend that everything is okay.
   E. Avoid the coworker as much as possible.

6. When you disagree with your team, you:
   A. Stand by your conviction and don't back down.
   B. Try to convince the majority of the team that you are right.
   C. Ask for everyone's opinion and look for alternatives all can agree upon.
   D. Go along with the team.
   E. Don't participate in the discussions, but don't feel bound by their decisions.

7. When one person on the team disagrees with everyone else, you:
   A. Suggest the group move on without that person's agreement.
   B. Give the dissenting person an opportunity to express his or her view.
   C. Try to get a group discussion going to explore the opposing view.
   D. Suggest the group set aside the issue and move on to another topic.
   E. Don't get involved.

8. In handling conflict between group members, you:
   A. Anticipate areas of resistance and prepare responses prior to meeting.
   B. Ask members to suggest possible areas of compromise.
   C. Encourage the group to explore reasons for conflict and identify concerns.
   D. Try to promote harmony so friendly relations are maintained.
   E. Ask for an impartial arbitrator to make a decision.

9. If you see conflict emerging in your team, you:
   A. Push for a quick decision to avoid discussion.
   B. Move the discussion to a middle ground.
   C. Ask the group if they can see the conflict and what they want to do about it.
   D. Relieve the tension with humor.
   E. Stay out of it since it is not your concern.

10. In your view, the cause of conflict within teams is:
    A. Lack of clearly stated positions.
    B. Not being open to compromise.
    C. Having a win/lose perspective.
    D. Not being motivated to get along together.

E. Leaders being more interested in maintaining their own power positions.

Scoring:
Count the number of A, B, C, D, and E responses and write the total number of each below.

A _____   D _____

B _____   E _____

C _____

The letter for which you have the highest number of responses represents your *primary conflict style*. This is how you handle conflict when you feel comfortable with the situation, in control, emotionally uninvolved, not threatened.

The second highest number is your *secondary conflict style*. That is the style you use under stress or pressure of conflict. You may use up your preferred style in the conflict, and as time drags on and emotions become involved, you cease to find that style effective. That is when you default to your backup style. For example, you may handle conflict at work in your primary style—collaborator—but as the conflict escalates, you may switch to being a withdrawer.

If you have big gaps between the totals of your scores, you may be locked into one style. If your totals are close, it means you often switch from one style to another.

If most of your responses are A: This indicates the *controller* style of handling conflict. Your primary goal is to win the conflict. You're usually convinced you are right and have little difficulty in telling others why they should do it your way. You may be directive in your approach to conflict without too much concern for the feelings of others. Controllers can be powerful, factual, forceful, exploding, stubborn, defending, decisive, resisting, demanding, right, and convincing.

If most of your responses are B: You tend to utilize the *accommodator* style of handling conflict. You are willing to lose a little if the other side loses a little too. You can see both sides of the issue and may be viewed by others as vacillating and unable to make a decision. Accommodators can be challenging, compromising, negotiating, distracting, smoothing, logical, communicating, planning, listening, giving, and democratic.

If most of your responses are C: You favor the *collaborator* style of handling conflict. Your goal is to achieve a win/win resolution. You are willing to take time to work through the conflict and listen to all sides of the issue. You are often asked to be an arbitrator in workplace conflict situations. Collaborators can be serious, committed, accepting, expressive, exploring, evaluating, sharing, sympathetic, open, collaborating, and searching.

If most of your responses are D: You have adopted an *appeaser* style of handling conflict. Your goal is to end the conflict, and if you have to give in to do so, you are willing to be the loser. Your primary concern is to keep the other side happy, and you often sacrifice your own feelings in order to bring the conflict to an end. Appeasers can be frightening (if their real agenda is hidden behind their seeming appeasement), emotional, supporting, quiet, compensating, following, harmonizing, peacemaking, placating, caring, and empathetic.

If most of your responses are E: An *avoider* style of handling conflict is your choice. You don't care who wins or loses, but tend to excuse yourself from the battlefield. You will withdraw emotionally or physically or both from the situation. Avoiders can be apathetic, uninterested, impersonal, withdrawing, nonparticipatory, silent, judging, unemotional, removing, impartial, and depressed.

Appropriate Times to Use the Five Styles

Each style has its merits and is appropriate in specific situations. Here are some examples.

Controller

 when a decision has to be made quickly
 when you are right and need closure
 when an unpopular issue must be resolved

Accommodator

 when the need for harmony is high
 when others need to learn through mistakes
 when you are wrong

Collaborator

 when there is mutual respect between parties
 when there is ample time to resolve the conflict
 when a long-term solution is required

Withdrawer

 when you need to buy time, but not to avoid problems
 when you want to slow down momentum and cool emotions

Appeaser

 when it is important to maintain trust on both sides
 when the issue isn't personally important to you

Self-awareness is your greatest asset when dealing with conflict. When you understand how you handle conflict, particularly which style you use when under pressure, you have an option to change your conflict style. As you engage in conflict, consider the style of your opponent. If he is a controller, your controller style will simply put the two of you in a quarrel. Instead try switching to a collaborator style to encourage your opponent to back down from the controller position. However, you must also realize that using a collaborative conflict style presupposes you have time to work through the issue and that there is mutual trust on each side. Otherwise, little will change.

Many managers don't see themselves as controllers; however, controlling behavior may be the reason that you have conflict in your workplace.

HOW CONTROLLING ARE YOU?

Directions: Mark all the statements that are usually true for you.

_____ 1. I tend to stay aloof from conversations, and if pressed, give one- or two-word answers.

_____ 2. I dominate meetings with my opinions and ideas.

_____ 3. I often offer unsolicited advice to employees and then get upset when they don't take it.

_____ 4. I am usually the last to apologize in an argument.

_____ 5. I give people the silent treatment when I'm angry or upset with them.

_____ 6. I make promises and then don't keep them.

_____ 7. When I want something done, I want it done *now*.

_____ 8. I am known for being late for appointments, and I frequently keep employees waiting.

_____ 9. I make social plans for the team without consulting them.

_____ 10. I tend to withhold information.

_____ 11. Others say that I don't listen.

_____ 12. If someone is telling a story or giving a presentation, I jump in and finish it for them.

_____ 13. I have to have the last word in an argument.

_____ 14. I am often critical of others.

_____ 15. When I want to get my point across, I raise my voice, even shout.

_____ 16. I have been accused of mumbling or talking too softly.

_____ 17. I ask employees how they want to handle a situation and then try to get them to do what I want.

_____ 18. I ask employees for ideas and then choose my own idea.

_____ 19. I insist on doing everything myself in order to have it done my way.

_____ 20. I withhold compliments and affirmations when I'm angry with an employee.

If you checked any of the following statements—2, 3, 4, 7, 8, 9, 12, 13, 14, 25, 17, and 19—you are an active controller in situations of conflict. People may be afraid of confronting you, may avoid getting into arguments with you, and may bury their negative feelings toward you rather than deal with your controlling behavior. As a manager, conflict in your workplace goes underground and results in low morale, sabotaged work, and negativity.

If you checked any of the following statements—1, 5, 6, 10, 11, 16, 18, and 20—you are a passive controller in situations of conflict. People may see you as moody, hard to read, difficult to communicate with, and dangerous to cross. As a manager, conflict in your workplace is likely to suddenly erupt, much to your surprise. You are unlikely to take any responsibility for the conflict.

Before you begin to work through a conflict, start by determining the source. Does the workplace environment play a part? Are employees suffering from too much pressure, too much competition, unrealistic expectations?

Sometimes just introducing a bit of fun into the workplace will ease tensions. If you can, relax a deadline, try to cut down on overtime, or spend more time giving your team members positive reinforcement. Some managers have found that team-building sessions greatly reduce tension and conflicts in the workplace.

If you feel that your workplace itself is not the source of conflict, there may be other causes.

OTHER SOURCES OF CONFLICT

Interpersonal Conflict

A potential for conflict exists simply because people are different. Differences in age, gender, beliefs, values, experience, and training give everyone a unique view on life or "perceptual set." A young, aggressive, formally trained employee will see things differently from an older employee who came up through the ranks. Normally you don't have a choice about whom you manage; therefore, if your employees are markedly different from you, you have the potential for conflict. Referring back to the SPOT profile in chapter 7, you can see how emotional issues might arise when people who are task-oriented are in conflict with people who are relationship-oriented.

Another source of interpersonal conflict is in the allocation of resources within an organization. Whether it is money, people, or equipment, someone has to decide who gets what. Competition is inevitable. People want what they perceive as their fair share. But their fair share may not be what others think is fair. The have-nots become antagonistic to those who they believe got more or to the person who allocated the resources.

Organizational Conflict

Conflicts can happen simply because of the structure of the organization. The them-and-us attitude is based on workers' perceptions that management has different organizational interests than they do. This is especially true in organizations with a union influence. What managers want may not be what workers want. You may need your group to work overtime on the weekend for a rush order, but they have already worked overtime during the week and want the weekend off. If you insist that they work the overtime, be aware of the underlying anger and distrust that comes from your dictatorial stance. Or, the union may prevent your using your positional authority, which leads to anger and distrust toward the union members.

Interdepartmental conflict also exists in many organizations. Different departments have different needs depending on what they have to accomplish. For example, sales may want to increase the volume of sales, but production cannot meet the demand without decreasing quality. The two departments disagree on goals. This type of conflict is widespread in organizations. The safety department wants small appliances moved out of offices because of the fear of a fire hazard. But those who work in the office resent not being able to brew coffee or warm up lunches. The problem with all these types of conflict isn't so much that they exist but that they are often neglected or ignored.

Add to these basic sources of conflict the daily annoyances and frustrations of the workplace that lead to misunderstandings based on age, race, or cultural differences; misplaced loyalties toward other employees, managers, or departments; perceived threats to security, power, or status; and competition that has gotten out of control. As a manager, you'll also have to deal with intolerance, prejudice, discrimination, or bigotry among employees; malicious rumors and gossip about an individual or a group;

long-standing grudges; workplace romances gone awry; finger-pointing and blaming; and alcohol- or drug-induced irrational behaviors.

The behaviors in the workplace that result from all these factors can range from shouting matches, name-calling, and vicious verbal exchanges; to sabotage and destruction of property; to actual violence. Escalating conflict can cause behaviors as simple as crying, sulking, or throwing tantrums; to work slowdown, refusal to cooperate, and refusal to communicate; to harassment, stalking, and physical threats.

It makes a manager wonder why she ever thought the job was worth doing.

What happens if you decide to ignore the conflict?

Conflicts can grow so overwhelming that the participants have no energy for their work. Two managers can spend so much time plotting to make the other look bad that the work doesn't get done.

Conflict can create so many interpersonal hostilities and negative feelings that people cannot bear to work with each other. Perhaps someone was passed over for promotion and now has to show you, the new manager, how to do your job. Frustration, jealousy, and anger could easily cause the passed-over person to gradually refuse to cooperate with you. Then others in the department will begin to take sides in the dispute.

Some conflict is so serious that the only way it can be resolved in the view of the combatants is for one of them to leave. This kind of all-or-nothing conflict is devastating to everyone involved; people can be demotivated and demoralized by it, and work suffers accordingly.

Even mild conflict has disadvantages. People may choose to bury a potential conflict in the hope that it will resolve itself. Usually the conflict reappears in a more virulent form as an adjunct to a completely different issue.

Conflict needs to be resolved. Not only does it make a difference to the morale and spirit of the workplace, but also it leads to other positive outcomes.

POSITIVE OUTCOMES OF CONFLICT
Despite all the potential negative consequences of conflict, positive outcomes are possible, depending on how the conflict is handled.

Promotes Creativity
Conflict can lead to innovation and creativity; new ideas often emerge from the clash of opinions—if the parties listen to each other and build on one another's ideas.

Is a paintbrush a pump, a spreader, or a hydraulic system? A group could spend a great deal of time arguing about that before coming up with a radical new design for a painting system, provided they listen to and understand one another's arguments and build on that understanding to create a new way to think about painting.

Increases Cooperation
Instead of creating differences, conflict can be the cause of cooperation if properly channeled. When the parties achieve a negotiated result that everyone can live with, the members learn the benefit of cooperation, which can lessen later conflicts or improve how they are dealt with. This is often the case in a union negotiation with management, when both sides have achieved some of their goals and have compromised to meet the agreement together. If the negotiation was fair and equable, union and management learn to trust each other and work together.

Improves Problem Solving
As people learn how to negotiate, everyone is more apt to benefit from the outcome. When people see that it is all right to disagree if the ultimate

goal is to negotiate a solution that everyone can live with, they also learn that disagreement can lead to creative problem solving that may bring about a solution that is better than their original perceived outcomes.

BEHAVIORS TO AVOID IN CONFLICT

When handling conflict, you'll want to keep in mind some behaviors to avoid. In and of themselves, they seem harmless enough, but when enacted within the context of interpersonal conflict, they can cause the conflict to escalate.

1. Don't take sides if the conflict is between two other parties. Most people have a bias, and you are no exception. Regardless of how you feel toward the employees, the issue, or the outcome, try to remain neutral.
2. Don't assume that the conflict will resolve itself. That rarely happens.
3. Don't assign blame. The resulting resentment can create further conflict down the line.
4. Don't treat the two sides like children, even if their behavior seems childish to you. You can't expect them to apologize either, and an apology shouldn't be a prerequisite for solving the problem.
5. Don't deal with the conflict in public. Most people need to save face, and if forced to back down publicly, they may dig in their heels on other issues.

THE EMOTION FACTOR

When human beings work together to complete tasks, emotions play a role. It is unrealistic to suppose that emotions can be checked at the door when you arrive at work. As a manager, you may believe that emotional neutrality is necessary, and you may try to hide your feelings from those around you. However, you'll probably be seen by your staff and coworkers as rigid, cold, unfeeling, detached, or fearful. If you keep yourself aloof and don't participate fully in the life of the workplace, they won't be able to develop the trust in you that is necessary for a collaborative approach to solving conflict.

Emotional intelligence (EI) is a behavioral model that rose to prominence with Daniel Goleman's 1995 book of the same name.[1] Originally developed in the 1970s and '80s by psychologists Howard Gardner, Peter Salovey, and John Mayer, this theory states that emotions are always present, so we must deal with them intelligently.

Essentially the premise of EI is that to be successful, you must be able to understand yourself—your goals, your intention, your responses, your behavior, and your emotions. As well, you need to understand the feelings and emotional responses of others.

When you are dealing with conflict, understanding what is happening to you and to the other person or persons on an emotional level gives you the insight into how to deal with the conflict in a positive way.

Mindful Handling of Conflict

How does a mindful manager deal with conflict? Here are some final thoughts to help you make the most of a difficult workplace situation.

Begin with prayer. Ask your higher power to help you acknowledge the emotions you are feeling about the conflict. Name them. Do you feel sad? Angry? Disappointed? Surprised? Fearful?

Now ask God to show you why you are feeling this way. Often the reason for an emotion goes beyond the current circumstance and is based on an event or experience that has nothing to do with what you are facing in the workplace.

Take time to examine the reason. Explore the feelings fully. Now ask

God to go back to that time or experience that triggered the emotion and to stand between you and whatever caused your feelings. God is timeless and able to redeem anything that happened to you in your past.

Thank God for loving you in that past time. Let the feelings go and picture the Spirit filling you with love and light instead.

Now ask God to help you understand the feelings of the other person. Consider what past events might have colored the situation for him. Pray earnestly for that person, asking God to free him from the events or experiences that might have added to the present conflict. Thank God for loving the person. Don't worry if you don't feel that love for him yourself right now. God knows your sincere desire to resolve the conflict. Finally, ask God to be present with you as you handle the conflict situation.

Now you are ready to move on to using the techniques that have been discussed in earlier chapters. Listen carefully to what the other person is saying. Use all the listening skills you have to hear beyond the words. Use assertive language to tell your side of the story. Finish with the EASY process (Express, Address, Suggest, Yes; see pages 143–44) to help reach consensus and resolution to the conflict. Always be mindful of God being present with you as you engage in working out the conflict.

The hardest job for a mindful manager is dealing with conflict in the workplace. Many managers feel guilty about conflict that may arise, particularly if the conflict is with someone they don't particularly like. People are people anywhere—some of them will be upset, angry, or frustrated. How you respond to them is critical.

If you remain mindful as you manage others, if you pray for each situation and the people involved in it, and if you depend upon God for wisdom, you will be in a position to handle your workplace conflict with power and grace.

PART FOUR

LEARNING NEW STRATEGIES

OLD WORLD MAPS USUALLY showed areas that were still unexplored. Sometimes those areas were marked with "Here there be dragons." As a manager today, you are going to find yourself moving into unexplored territory, full of unknown dangers and pitfalls. Here are some indications that you have reached dragon territory.

- You have trouble making decisions. You find yourself waffling back and forth from one alternative to the other. Even when you make a decision, you continue to second-guess yourself.
- You experience conflicting emotions. One minute, you feel excited, even elated, about your job; the next minute, you feel scared, worried, even angry with the job.

- You feel overwhelming fatigue. Everything seems to require too much effort. You find it hard to keep your momentum going. Just the thought of continuing through the challenges and difficulties of your job makes you tired.
- You experience a loss of control. You feel like you are on an express train heading into a dark tunnel. There is no way you can stop the train, and you are not sure what is at the other end of the tunnel.
- You have a lingering sense of fear. Deep inside, you wonder where this will all end. You know there are dragons out there, but you are not sure if you have the ability to fight them all.

At this precarious point in your life as a manager, God can begin to work with you powerfully. As you are mindful of God's presence, the dragons that once seemed so huge and threatening simply disappear in the light of your new ways of thinking and managing.

11

LEADING BY EMPOWERING OTHERS

Leadership is the most important managerial function you will ever learn. The way you lead your employees determines the success of your team, division, and total organization. Leadership involves knowing your employees and what motivates them. It means knowing the group dynamics of your work unit. It is the ability to lead, plan, direct, organize, inspire, motivate, learn, teach, train, resolve conflicts, build an effective team, and keep performance high.

Your employees are people who are more experienced and less experienced, older and younger, of the same gender and of the opposite gender, friends and foes. Their enthusiasm for the job ranges from burned-out to turned-on to just plain disinterested. Somehow you must find a way to light a fire within them that will continue to fuel itself. How do you get your team motivated? How do you light that internal fire? The key is empowerment.

To *empower* means to enable, allow, or permit. There are two aspects to organizational empowerment:

1. Building, developing, and increasing power through cooperation, sharing, and working together.
2. Making a commitment to common goals, taking risks, and demonstrating initiative and creativity.

Empowerment encourages your employees to participate actively in the decision-making process. It allows them to achieve recognition, involvement, and a sense of worth in their jobs, thus improving job satisfaction and morale.

EMPOWERING OTHERS THROUGH LEADERSHIP

What's Your Leadership Style? A Self-Test
Directions: Read each statement below and rate yourself from 1 to 5, with 1 being "very much like me" (or strongly agree), to 5 being "not at all like me" (or strongly disagree).

1. I should be setting the goals for my group. I know what needs to be done, how to do it, and what resources we have. 1 2 3 4 5
2. If subordinates would take the time to listen more carefully to instructions, there wouldn't be so many problems on the job. 1 2 3 4 5
3. I am the manager of my group because my skills and experience make me an expert at what we do. 1 2 3 4 5
4. It is not my job to worry about the personal problems of my employees. They should leave their personal problems at home. 1 2 3 4 5
5. Sometimes it is necessary to get tough with employees in order to get the job done. 1 2 3 4 5
6. I don't worry about whether or not my team likes what I am doing. That is their problem, not mine. 1 2 3 4 5

7. I take credit for what gets accomplished in my department. That is my job as manager—to get things done. 1 2 3 4 5
8. I don't have a problem using my authority when I want to get something done. 1 2 3 4 5
9. As a manager I should get to enjoy a few extra perks, such as a reserved parking space, bigger office, or expensive trips. 1 2 3 4 5
10. It is not my job to provide counseling to my employees. That is why we have a human resources department. 1 2 3 4 5
11. I prefer to take care of any problems that arise in our group by myself. That is my job. 1 2 3 4 5
12. I don't mind telling people what they have to do. I can lay things out for them and tell them to do it. 1 2 3 4 5
13. I make well-thought-out plans for my group and expect them to carry out those plans. 1 2 3 4 5
14. If I want input from my group, I will ask them for it. It is a waste of my time to listen to a lot of ideas that aren't relevant to what we are doing right now. 1 2 3 4 5
15. I believe that the company's appraisal and feedback system is all I need to use to tell my employees how they are doing. 1 2 3 4 5

Scoring: Add all your scores and indicate the total here _____. If your total score is:

15–25: You tend to be an *authoritarian* leader in your style.

26–50: You tend to be a *consultative* leader.

51–75: You are most likely a *facilitative* leader.

Authoritarian Leader

Authoritarian leaders provide clear expectations to group members on what should be done, when it should be completed, and how it should be accomplished.

Authoritarian leaders make decisions without input from group members. Overuse of an authoritarian style can be construed as bossy and controlling. Worst-case examples of this style can be seen when leaders utilize bullying techniques, such as yelling, abusing power, or demeaning group members.

This style has been greatly criticized during the past thirty years. If you have Gen-X staff (those born from 1965 to 1982), they will be highly resistant to the authoritarian style. Generally speaking, an authoritarian style will often result in low staff morale and high turnover, absenteeism, and work stoppage. The authoritarian style does not empower others.

Consultative Leader

Consultative managers exercise little control over their groups, leaving them to sort out their own roles and tackle their work on their own. In general, this approach leaves the team floundering, with little direction or motivation.

The Roman Empire used this kind of management style with the various consuls and representatives it sent to the far-flung reaches of its empire. In Jesus' time, Pontius Pilate, as the representative of Rome, was not required to seek permission from his superiors for his judgments or actions.

But there are situations where the consultative approach can be effective. The consultative technique is usually appropriate when leading a team of highly motivated and skilled people who have produced excellent work in the past.

Facilitative Leader

Facilitative leaders accept input from one or more group members when making decisions and solving problems, but the leader retains the final say when choices are made. Group members tend to be encouraged and motivated by this style of leadership. Facilitative management is not presiding or presenting information, relegating or controlling, solving other people's problems or making decisions for them.

Whatever leadership style they use, mindful managers coach and enable others to act. In order to empower people, managers become leaders/facilitators.

Moving from a controlling to a more facilitative style of leadership means you change the way you accomplish your work, change how you conduct relationships with your staff, change your behavior, and change your communication style and mind-set.

What can you expect to happen as you learn to lead as a facilitator? Getting employees to accept change may take time. Don't expect others to welcome your first attempts to become a leader/facilitator. Your employees may be suspicious and antagonistic to any change in the way things are done. When you first begin to draw people out, listen to them more carefully, and ask for their input, they may be wary and afraid to open up. Your task will be to earn their trust. You will do that by telling the truth, even when it is difficult, and being authentic and trustworthy in your dealings with your staff.

FIVE SKILLS OF A LEADER/FACILITATOR

1. Discover Personal Strengths of Team Members
The best teams are made up of individuals who do not think alike. Effective teams have members with different talents, backgrounds, cultures, education, life skills, and work skills. The skilled leader/facilitator actively seeks different points of view and differences in opinions that will

enhance the overall knowledge of the team. By asking for opinions and listening to others' viewpoints, the manager begins to understand the specialized knowledge or interests of the team that may not be apparent in day-to-day interactions.

2. Keep an Open Mind

People often make assumptions about others based on their appearance or behavior. Managers get into trouble when they begin to think of these assumptions as facts. When you make snap judgments or attribute negative thoughts or motives to others, you limit your ability to develop positive relationships or work effectively with them.

What can you do to limit the assumptions you make about members of your work team? Be aware of how and when you are making assumptions. Recognize that your assumptions aren't necessarily based on facts. Realize that others may be making assumptions that are different from your own.

Take responsibility for checking your assumptions with others on the team. You might say, "I'd like to review how we made this decision. I'm assuming that those who didn't speak up are comfortable with it. If that's not true, I'd like to revisit the way we make decisions in the group and find ways to include everyone's opinion."

3. Actively Listen

Skilled leader/facilitators listen not only to the words of employees but also to the manner and tone in which the words are spoken. They draw out each team member, making sure everyone has the opportunity to participate. Some team members don't say what they think. They may be timid or afraid of revealing an unpopular opinion. They need to be reassured and empowered.

4. Trust, Even with Risk

Once the groundwork is laid, facilitators must trust their staff. None of the other skills matter if the leader doesn't trust the process and the people. If you say, "Well, that was an interesting discussion, but here's what I've decided to do," your staff will lose confidence and won't take ownership for the work of the team. Give staff members ownership of their tasks. Allow them to make mistakes or do the work differently than you would. If you trust them, they'll prove they deserve it.

5. Give Credit where Due

It is always unwise for a leader to take credit for work done by the team. Members lose heart quickly if they feel they are being treated unfairly. To be effective in empowering others, make sure that the work and results are credited both to the department as a whole and to individual employees.

Wise leaders know that instead of giving up power, sharing it means that they are actually expanding their power.

EMPOWERING OTHERS THROUGH DELEGATION

Delegation, as an empowering tool, is the act of assigning and entrusting responsibilities to others. Delegating is not about giving people tasks to do. Tasks are the simple and short-term items of work to be done. Delegating is about having your staff take on meaningful work—projects, duties, and other important assignments.

Entrust is a key word in delegating; it means that you care about the results of what you delegate, and you are willing to provide the support needed to accomplish the task.

Delegation—A Self-Test

Directions: Read each of the following statements. Circle A = *always*, S = *sometimes*, or N = *never* as your response to this statement:

I don't delegate because . . .

A   S   N   I'm new at this job.

A   S   N   I can do it better myself.

A   S   N   I don't have time to explain it to someone else.

A   S   N   I don't want someone else to mess it up.

A   S   N   I love getting right into the job.

A   S   N   I don't like giving up authority.

A   S   N   I'm afraid people won't like me if I give them work.

A   S   N   I'm afraid I won't be needed if I delegate the work.

A   S   N   I tried to delegate, but the worker refused the task.

A   S   N   All my people are already overworked.

A   S   N   I'm always under deadline pressure. I don't have time to delegate.

A   S   N   I feel uncomfortable if something is happening that I'm not involved in.

A   S   N   I have to redo work that isn't up to my standards.

A   S   N   I wish people would be more proactive and volunteer to do things.

A   S   N   I don't have time to oversee the job if someone else is doing it.

Scoring:

Add all your A responses and multiply by 5: #As _____ x 5 = _____

Add all your S responses and multiply by 3: #Ss _____ x 3 = _____

Add all your N responses and multiply by 1: #Ns _____ x 1 = _____

Total the three scores here: Total score: _____

    If you scored less than 30, you are great at delegating.

    If you scored between 31 and 59, you are inconsistent at delegating.

    If you scored over 60, you need to learn how to let go.

Why Managers Fail to Delegate

1. New to Management

People who are newly promoted to managerial positions may have trouble delegating. They were promoted because they are good at what they do. They try to keep doing the previous job rather than developing new subordinates to do that job. They are used to doing all the tasks and find it hard to relinquish them.

2. "I Can Do It Better Myself"

Maybe you can. That isn't the point. Delegate because your choice is between (a) doing a better job on this one item, or (b) planning, developing, supervising, and training a team. Eventually anyone on your team should be able to do the job better than you.

3. Lack of Time

Delegating tasks takes time. In the early stages, train people to take over tasks. It might be quicker to do the task yourself than delegate it and coach the other person, but in time your coaching investment pays off. People will learn to do tasks with minimum supervision and assistance.

4. Fear of Mistakes

Just as you have to develop staff to do tasks without your involvement, you will have to let people make mistakes—and then help them correct them. Most people soon learn to do jobs properly.

5. "I Enjoy Getting My Hands Dirty"

By doing jobs yourself you will probably get them done effectively. If your assistants are standing idle while you do this, however, your department will be seriously inefficient. Think of the cost of your time and your department's time when you're tempted to do a job yourself.

6. Fear of Surrendering Authority

Whenever you delegate, you must surrender some authority but not responsibility. Remember your ultimate goal: by effective delegation, you get adequate time to do your more important work well.

7. Insecurity

Are you afraid your subordinates won't like you if you delegate work to them? Are you afraid you'll look like the person who isn't needed? Too often, managers won't delegate because of a sense of personal insecurity. Keep reminding yourself that delegation is an expression of your belief in both the ability of others to perform the task, and of yourself to let go of the task.

8. Workers Lack Skills or Desire

Maybe the person you selected for the job doesn't have the skills, knowledge, or experience to do it. Perhaps the employee is trying to avoid responsibility. You will have to deal with this attitude. By providing training, beginning with small tasks, and being patient, you'll build skill, competence, and confidence. Be firm but reasonable.

9. Staff Is Overworked

If everyone is working at full capacity, consider outsourcing the job. If this can't be done, check the workloads and habits of each person working for you. Is each using time efficiently? Is each delegating tasks to support staff? Are any tasks being done that are outdated, redundant, or unnecessary?

WHY DELEGATE?

No matter how productive you think you are, you are human and have limits. Delegating gets others to share your goals and support your work. Effective delegating shows you are ready to take on more responsibility.

The president of the company doesn't answer the phones and open the mail. These tasks, and many more, are delegated to others. When you delegate, you groom your successor. When you move up, someone will be ready to replace you. As you share power, you create more for yourself and others.

You can accomplish more if you have a bigger sphere of control and productivity. More work is seen streaming through your office. You get more done in the same time. You are working smarter, not harder.

Delegating does *not* mean giving up responsibility. When you delegate a task, you are still responsible for it. Ask for periodic progress reports. Monitor the work, but give the employee freedom to perform it on her own.

Delegating *does* mean you work more effectively by letting others help with tasks. It also allows them to demonstrate their abilities and initiative. Grant the authority employees need to accomplish a task, and then allow them to make decisions.

Delegating also means allowing people to learn from their mistakes and become better workers. You don't have to accept late or shoddy work. You do have to show the person how and why the work is not up to standard, and direct him along a better route to success.

How to Delegate

When faced with a task that could be delegated to another, ask yourself these questions:

1. Am I the only one who can do this?
2. If yes, why do I believe that to be true?
3. If I am not the only one who can do this, why am I doing it?
4. What would motivate someone else to take this on?
5. What is the worst that could happen if she makes a mistake?

Empowering Others through Decision Making: A Self-Test

How do you make decisions in the workplace? Take this quiz and find out. For each question, circle the letter of the answer that best describes your workplace practices.

1. When I have to set goals for our department, I:
    A. Let my superiors make the decisions and set the goals.
    B. Decide on the goals for my department with little input from anyone else.
    C. Tell my staff what the goals are and ask them to vote on them.
    D. Ask my staff to give me ideas and input for the goals we should set.

2. When I have to deal with a conflict that involves my whole staff, I:
    A. Refer the matter to the human resources department.
    B. Lay down the law and tell the various factions what I expect.
    C. Side with the majority, because I feel that is the fairest way to solve the problem.
    D. Take time to sit down with all concerned and work with them until we can mutually agree to a solution.

3. When I need to fire a staff member, I:
    A. Give my boss the particulars and let her deal with the issue.
    B. Begin termination proceedings.
    C. Use the rules and regulations of the company to back up my decision.
    D. Talk it over with my peers and comanagers and ask what they would do.

4. When I have to make a tough budget decision, I:
   A. Wait and see what the finance department has to say.
   B. Make the decision and let the chips fall where they may.
   C. Get my staff together and let them vote on the various items.
   D. Ask everyone to hand in a budget report for their particular needs and then work on the budget as a group.

5. When I have a big project coming up that requires extra help, I:
   A. Stay late and do the job myself.
   B. Choose who will work and inform them.
   C. Ask people to volunteer to work overtime.
   D. Explain the project and ask the staff how we can get it done.

Scoring: Add up the total number of times you circled each letter, and indicate those totals here.

A _____ B _____ C _____ D _____

There are a number of methods for making decisions. The style you choose depends to a great extent on the importance of the decision to be made, whether it requires wide acceptance, and how much time is available to make the decision.

If most of your answers are A: Your decision-making style is *abdication*. Avoiding the problem and hoping it will simply disappear is one way of making a decision, but it is not recommended. There may be occasions when failure to act is a reasonable solution, but if it happens too often, it could be a sign that the team is not working well together and not fulfilling its responsibilities.

If most of your answers are B: Your decision-making style is *autonomy*. A decision may be made by a leader when fast action is required or when the decision does not affect all members of the team. If this kind of action is taken too often, however, the rest of the team may feel shut out of decision making and will be less likely to give support later.

If most of your answers are C: Your decision-making style is *majority rule*. When a decision must be made quickly and there is no time to get the full consensus of the group, the team is asked to vote, and the majority rules. Even though team members may be consulted and allowed to speak for and against the solution, the majority rule method has some obvious pitfalls:

- Some members don't speak up, and the decision isn't informed by their experience and knowledge.
- Team members who vote against the decision may not feel a commitment to supporting it. People sometimes go away from the meeting dissatisfied with both the decision and the process.

Majority rule is a quick and easy method to arrive at a decision. If this method is used, it is important that team members agree ahead of time that everyone will support it.

If most of your answers are D: Your decision-making style is *consensus*. This method is used when full support is critical and team members have considerable time to ensure all parties support the final decision.

A consensus process generates a wide range of ideas and options. It works best when there is already a high degree of agreement and cohesiveness among team members. The essential ingredient is openness—the ability to listen to each other, the willingness to offer honest opinions and new ideas, and the capacity to change one's mind after hearing the ideas and opinions expressed by others on the team.

How can a leader/facilitator help the team build trust in order to make a decision by consensus?

- Allow time for the team members to get to know one another.
- Encourage members to talk about their backgrounds, past jobs, and any experiences that relate to the work of the team.
- Find out what each member needs in order to feel a significant part of the whole.
- Spend time coming to an agreement on the purpose and importance of the decision to be made.
- Make sure everyone understands the outcome of making a decision.
- Acknowledge all ideas as potentially valid.

A mindful manager asks open-ended questions and actively listens to the answers. (An open-ended question cannot be answered with a yes or no; it usually starts with *how*, *why*, and *what*.) Keep an open mind. Don't judge or criticize. Actively draw out ideas, opinions, and concerns. Coach and nurture without telling your employees how or what to do. Try to encourage different viewpoints. Help the group to reach agreement on the best course of action.

EMPOWERING OTHERS THROUGH MEETING THEIR NEEDS

You can empower employees by being aware of and responding to the particular needs they bring with them to the workplace. Here are some of those needs.

1. Security

People with a high need for security are deeply affected by sudden changes, unforeseen events, real or perceived threats to their job, their livelihood, or their sense of self. Their fears may prevent them from functioning adequately, and they may react negatively to someone they feel is threatening their security.

Conversely, people whose need for security is low or who get bored easily may welcome change of any kind. A manager who thrives on change but has a staff with high security needs can create havoc.

2. Belonging

People who have a particular need for belonging are a valuable addition to any group. They are often a stabilizing presence and help others tolerate one another. They may go along with whatever proposals are made to avoid any conflict in a group. It is hard for them to express different opinions because of their fear of rejection. A person with a need for belonging needs to feel accepted, as well as to accept others. She can be seen as a doormat with no personal opinion, or her time may be abused, since she will rarely criticize others or say no.

3. Opportunities to Advance

People with a need for achievement will constantly try to expand their knowledge and the boundaries of that knowledge. This is good if they are in positions where that energy can be focused on assisting a company to grow, creating new knowledge, or creating new products. It can be bad if their only outlet for expansion is to take from others. When their need for expansion is thwarted, they may try to meet that need in inappropriate and harmful ways. They may poach on the work territory of others, take control whenever possible, and push themselves into the limelight at the expense of others, creating dissension and stress in the workplace. Others become guarded and jealous of their own small kingdoms.

4. Personal Power

People with a need for personal power may resist new rules. In an open environment, they may excel at projects that require or reward independent thinking and spontaneity. They help others learn to exercise independent judgment.

If you manage people with a need for personal power, you will get along best with them when you recognize and respect their ability to make choices for themselves.

5. Challenge
People who need to be challenged will lead the pack to find new things to do, new places to visit, new markets to open, new products to sell, new ways of doing things, new ways of organizing the company.

If things get boring, people with a need for challenge will find a way to liven them up—either in a positive way by initiating something new, or in negative ways by going off on their own, taking great risks, or criticizing others who don't need or want to be challenged.

6. Recognition
It is important for employees to know that you are aware of their existence, that you recognize them and remember their names. When managers fail to greet employees or respond to their greetings, it can lead to a high degree of demotivation, lack of trust, and disloyalty. Your regard for people shines through in all of your actions and words. Your facial expression, body language, and words express what you think about the people who report to you. Your goal is to demonstrate your appreciation for each person's unique value. No matter how an employee is performing on a current task, that employee should always know that you value him or her as a human. Use simple, powerful, motivational words to demonstrate that you value the people you work with. Don't forget to say, "Please," "Thank you," and "You're doing a good job."

The Affirmation Principle: Tell Me I'm Okay

Mindful managers are careful to affirm each employee. They catch them doing things right and tell them so. They compliment them on their work, their dress, their attitude, their strengths. One caution: phony compliments will be spotted instantly. If you look regularly, you will find good work to compliment honestly. If you regularly give employees positive feedback, when you need to point out opportunities for improvement, your criticism will be better received.

Make it your goal to start every day with a positive affirmation for your entire staff. Your arrival and the first moments you spend with staff each day have an immeasurable impact on employee motivation and morale. Start the day right. Smile. Stand tall and confidently. Walk around your workplace and greet people. Share the goals and expectations for the day. Let the staff know that today is going to be a great day. It starts with you. Tell them it's going to be okay.

Employees are enabled when you give them permission to participate in workplace decisions; committed when you create opportunities for personal expression; and productive when you encourage them, listen to them, and give them feedback.

Mindful managers are empowered by God. Through that divine power, you are able to let go of your grip on autocratic power and give personal power to your employees. Your belief in a higher power allows you to move from the lip service of empowerment to active participation in delegation, decision sharing, and group responsibility. When you recognize the truth of God with you in your workplace, you can become an empowering manager.

FINDING GOD-GIFTED WAYS TO LOOK AT OLD CHALLENGES

Companies pay a great deal of money to bring in consultants and experts to show their people how to think outside the box. Unfortunately these gurus seldom explain what's inside the box, or how it became a box in the first place.

Think of the box as a flattened square with four sides, rather than as a cube. Each side of the square represents a set of templates you carry in your head. These templates determine how you react to situations, your perception of the present reality, and your concerns about the future. Together they limit the number of options available to you when you encounter a challenge.

Thinking inside the box is simply limited thinking. Once you get away from those templates and go outside—even beyond—the box, your options expand greatly.

Side 1: Rules

Do you remember your first day of school? The teacher gave you a big sheet of paper with a picture on it and a brand-new box of crayons. Eagerly you picked up the purple crayon and began to color the sky. Immediately the teacher told you that the sky wasn't purple but blue. So you colored in the sky area of the picture with your new blue crayon, exuberantly sweeping the crayon from side to side with little regard for the lines. "Stay inside the lines. The lines are our friends," the teacher told you. So you reined in your enthusiasm and began to carefully color within the designated lines. It wasn't as much fun, but the teacher was happy and praised your efforts. You just learned the "rules":

1. There is one right way to do things. All other ways are wrong.
2. Someone else will tell you which is the right way.
3. If you do it the wrong way, you'll get in trouble.
4. If you do it the right way, you'll be praised.

Side 2: Patterns

Most of us have certain patterns of thinking that we adopt to face any situation. It's called the "I always" response. Just listen to people around you talk about their lives. "I always get mad when I have to work overtime." "I always point out the negative aspects first." "I always keep my mouth shut in meetings." "I always end up with the most work to do."

Patterned thinking is an easy way out. You don't have to think about what you are doing—it is now a habit. If you always react negatively to something, don't worry—you know exactly how you will react to it the next time it comes down the pike.

SIDE 3: BELIEFS

Your beliefs are subtle inner messages that tell you how to behave in situations. They were ingrained in you during your earliest childhood years, coming from the adults around you. Those adults told you what kind of person you were ("Don't be such a crybaby!"), how you should respond ("Don't talk to strangers"), and what you should do ("Always be polite to adults"). Unfortunately, when you were a child, your brain didn't have the ability to filter out untrue or unrealistic statements. Instead you took them all at face value and created a belief system that now forms part of your thinking box.

You'll always know when you're operating under one of your beliefs. You'll find yourself saying the word *should*.

> "I should have seen that problem coming and prepared for it."
> "I should have told him what I really thought about it."
> "I should have started on this project weeks ago."

It's called "shoulding" all over yourself. It means that you know what it is that you "should" do, but you don't do it. Most of your "shoulds" will be a result of your core beliefs.

What Are Your Core Beliefs?

Directions: Circle the number after each of the following statements that indicates how strongly you believe the statement, with 1 being "strongly disagree" and 5 being "strongly agree."

1. When something doesn't work the way I think it should, it's usually someone else's fault. 1 2 3 4 5
2. Things would work out a lot better for me if I had a different boss or supervisor. 1 2 3 4 5

3. My opportunities in life are determined by the support or sabotage of others. 1 2 3 4 5

4. If I am unhappy with a situation, it is probably because someone else put me there. 1 2 3 4 5

5. The system is set up so that only the lucky people can get ahead. 1 2 3 4 5

6. I am uncomfortable with how far I have gotten in my life because I don't really think I deserve it. 1 2 3 4 5

7. Considering who I am, I am pretty lucky to have done as well as I have. 1 2 3 4 5

8. If people knew the real me, they wouldn't be so impressed with any success I have. 1 2 3 4 5

9. I find it hard to believe that people think I am capable and able to handle my job. 1 2 3 4 5

10. If I am honest, I don't consider myself to be a worthwhile or lovable person. 1 2 3 4 5

11. Most people are only concerned with themselves and never think about the other person. 1 2 3 4 5

12. I don't expect any great things in life; I have to be content with what I have. 1 2 3 4 5

13. I can't really trust anyone; trust only leaves a person open to betrayal. 1 2 3 4 5

14. People who talk about an abundant universe are starry-eyed fools. 1 2 3 4 5

15. I don't expect too much; that way I won't be disappointed. 1 2 3 4 5

16. When something unexpected occurs, it upsets me more than most people. 1 2 3 4 5

17. I hate it when I have to rearrange my schedule because something unexpected comes up. 1   2   3   4   5
18. Change usually means that everything is going to be more difficult than usual. 1   2   3   4   5
19. Once I have learned how to do something, I don't see any reason to change my methods. 1   2   3   4   5
20. People make changes because they are bored. If it's not broken, don't fix it. 1   2   3   4   5
21. No one can have what it takes to be successful in all areas of his or her life. 1   2   3   4   5
22. There are certain abilities that I know I don't have, and there is no point in trying to acquire them now. 1   2   3   4   5
23. It is luck, not ability, that determines a person's success in life, and I am just not lucky. 1   2   3   4   5
24. I am an average person, no different from anyone else.
    1   2   3   4   5
25. I know the things I can't do, and I make sure that I never get into a situation where I might have to learn to do them. 1   2   3   4   5

Add up your score for:

    Questions 1–5   _____

    Questions 6–10   _____

    Questions 11–15   _____

    Questions 16–20   _____

    Questions 21–25   _____

Out of a possible 25 for each section, a low score—13 and under—indicates that you have a positive core belief. A higher score—14 and above—indicates a negative core belief.

Questions 1–5: Personal Responsibility

How do you feel about taking responsibility for problems? Do you blame other people, other circumstances? Do you decide whose fault it is—his/hers/the system's? Are you like the four main characters in *The Wizard of Oz* who believed that someone or something else was responsible for their unhappiness? The lion couldn't be brave, the tin man couldn't be loving, the scarecrow couldn't be smart, and Dorothy couldn't find her way home. Why? Because someone hadn't given them courage, heart, brains to empower them. They were looking for someone else to take responsibility for their lives; they were looking for the wizard of Oz.

If you see yourself as a loved creation of God, you are more apt to take responsibility for your actions and trust that God will take care of any mistakes you may make.

Questions 6–10: Self-worth

Do you feel lovable? Do you feel deserving of good things in your life? Do you put yourself down? Call yourself stupid? Label yourself unworthy? Do you consistently remind yourself that you are worthless, useless, hopeless, and helpless?

If you see yourself as a loved creation of God, you know that you don't have to deserve the abundant life that is promised to you. It is given to you by divine grace.

Questions 11–15: Expectations

What is your expectation for your world? Do you feel that you are part of a supportive, benevolent universe? What about your life? Do you expect to succeed, live life fully, enjoy yourself? Do you believe that people are basically good and can be trusted? Is your core belief in your expectations of the world, your life, and your relationships positive and empowering or negative and debilitating?

If you see yourself as a loved creation of God, you know that creation would blossom with abundance if every person were to share with another.

Questions 16–20: Change

How do you feel about change? Do you get upset when something unexpected occurs? You may have a core belief that change is bad and that there is safety in what is known. Do you believe that you should stick with what you know, look before you leap, stay within the lines, and not make waves?

If you see yourself as a loved creation of God, you know that you don't have to fear change, because your security lies on the bedrock of God's unchanging character.

Questions 21–25: Personal Abilities

Do you feel that you have what it takes to be successful in all areas of your life? You core belief about your personal abilities is expressed as either "I can" or "I can't." When you are offered an opportunity to try something different, which of these is your first response?

If you see yourself as a loved creation of God, you know that you have been given the strengths and abilities you need to live your daily life.

SIDE 4: INITIATIVE

The final side of your thinking box deals with initiative. Do you feel life is good enough? Not bad? As well as can be expected under the circumstances?

Do you often answer questions with "okay"? For example:

"How's it going?"

"Okay."

"How's the department doing?"

"Okay."

Stay inside this box long enough and you'll end up with a tombstone that reads: "Here lies Joan. She lived an okay life."

You have been promised so much more in life than mediocrity. As a mindful manager, you can expect to go far beyond okay in your daily doings. God has called you to be exceptional. Anyone who has been told, "You have made them [human beings] a little lower than God, and crowned them with glory and honor" (Psalm 8:5), is not just okay. You are extraordinary and capable of doing extraordinary things.

What happens if you try to lead others from inside the box of your own thinking? Your leadership will be limited to only a few avenues of action—those dictated by the rules or the "right" way to do something, those dictated by how you always respond, and those dictated by what you believe you should do, but don't.

Then you tell yourself that it is okay, and you close the box and seal it.

Why would you do this? Because the box of thinking creates a comfort zone in your mind. Comfort zones are insidious simply because they are comfortable. When you are in one, it takes much effort to get out of it. The comfort zone becomes a comfortable rut in which you live your life—no surprises, no challenges, and no excitement. Sounds pretty good—until you realize that the only difference between a rut and a grave is about six feet!

Burst Out of the Box!

How do you burst out of the box of your own thinking? How do you escape the comfort zone that traps you into inaction? You use provocative thinking. To be provocative is to stir up purposely, to provoke, excite, stimulate, and call forth. Provocative thinking means that you will purposely stir up your thinking patterns and excite your imagination, thus stimulating and calling forth new ideas from deep within your creative self. You'll stir up the provocative thinking of your employees too, liberating them from the comfort zones of their thinking boxes.

In the same way, the prophets of the Old Testament—Jeremiah, Isaiah, Ezekiel, Daniel—brought provocative thinking to the people of Israel with their visions, their prophesies, and their messages from God. In later times, Jesus offered ideas, thoughts, and actions far beyond the inside-the-box thinking of the people around him. His ideas were disturbing, exciting, frightening, liberating, and thought-provoking.

In order to start breaking down the sides of your thinking box, forget about the rules. Look how far Jesus went outside the rules. He healed on the sabbath, talked with Samaritans, ate with the tax collectors, and touched the unclean.

Instead of always adhering to the rules, try going outside the box and looking for new ways to think. When faced with a problem, stop looking for *the* right answer and look for *another* right answer, and another and another. Try brainstorming, either alone or with your employees. In brainstorming, the only rule is that there are no rules. Anything goes—no matter how silly, how impossible, or how impractical. Let the ideas flow without censure or evaluation. If you have trouble starting a brainstorming session, play the "What if . . ." game. Simply postulate ridiculous scenarios involving the subject, and let your brain fill in the endless possibilities. You will be surprised at what good ideas lurk in your creative brain.

The next time you catch yourself saying, "I always . . . ," pinch yourself—hard. The pain will make you conscious of this habit that you use as a thinking crutch instead of learning new ways to deal with new situations.

Don't "should" on yourself. *Should* is a word that makes you feel powerless, helpless, and hopeless. There are no "shoulds" in God's love. Instead of looking back and continually second-guessing yourself, simply make your decision and move on. Remember, there is no single right way to do things, and your way may be the twenty-third right answer that no one has thought of before.

Finally, if you find yourself settling for mediocrity, you will know you just slipped into your comfort zone. It will feel good, but it is deadly.

As you begin to break down the sides of your thinking box, expect to feel uncomfortable. You are heading into dragon territory, that uncharted area on the map of your life marked, "Here there be dragons." You don't have to navigate this territory alone. Continually be aware of God with you as you burst out of the thinking box.

A final warning about provocative thinking: most people don't want their comfort zones to be disturbed. If you are using provocative thinking with your employees, be gentle. Give them time to get used to the idea that they won't be censured for crazy, off-the-wall ideas. It takes time, especially if thinking boxes have been the norm in your workplace.

Two Comfort Zones That Kill Creativity

1. That's Not the Way We Always Do It!

"The way it has always been done" is one of the most destructive comfort zones in the workplace. When members of your team come to you with an idea, have you found yourself saying, "We tried that once. It didn't work," or "It'll never be approved by the finance department," or "We've never done it this way"? These phrases are a surefire way to kill creativity and, at the same time, put down the person who dared to think outside the box.

2. That's Not My Job!

When a team sees itself as an isolated unit, it doesn't consider its impact on the organization as a whole. That's why it is important for your staff to see their place in the big picture of the organization. It's also important for your employees to see you doing some of the tough jobs, not just the interesting or challenging work. Getting down and dirty on the shop floor once in a while isn't a bad idea, and it lets your employees know that you all share responsibility to see a job through to completion.

FOUR DON'TS THAT KILL CREATIVITY

1. Don't Make Mistakes

Do you tend to remember your mistakes more than your successes? Do you worry about making a mistake when you have to try something you have never done before? Do you think about what can go wrong before you think about what can go right? Do you dislike having to learn something by trial and error?

If you answered yes to these four questions, you probably carry a don't-make-mistakes message in your head. You cautiously feel your way through each day, avoiding any risks that might lead to failure. You learn that the safest way to avoid mistakes is to stick to what you know works.

No doubt, your don't-make-mistakes message has been passed on subconsciously to your employees. This kind of thinking puts creativity under lock and key.

Before you can move beyond good enough to excellent, and from adequate to above expectations, you need to give yourself permission to make mistakes. Trust your higher power to bring good out of any mistakes you make. Admit to the mistake, ask for forgiveness, and move on.

In the same way, give your team members permission to make mistakes. Encourage them to try innovative approaches to their problems. Let them know that mistakes are okay and are part of the learning process.

Then stand back and watch what happens!

2. Don't Waste Time

Do you feel uncomfortable when you have nothing specific you need to do? Are you frustrated when people get off the subject in meetings? Do you try to use every minute in a structured way? Do you consider yourself a better time manager than most of the people you know?

If you answered yes to these questions, one of your credos is "Don't waste time." Your day planner may be meticulously filled in, with every minute accounted for and each appointment carefully planned. You may be proud of your time management abilities and consider it one of your strengths as a manager. Yet this same strength can be a weakness when it comes to dealing with your team.

When you look at each minute as being either useful or wasted, you are arbitrarily making a judgment. Standing in line at the bank may be a waste of time for you, yet for the person behind you, it is a golden opportunity to think through a problem. Getting off topic at the meeting may be annoying to you, yet to your employee it is the only way to bring a subject up for discussion. It is all a matter of learning to go with the flow.

This may seem a risky undertaking to you. It means giving up control of time when circumstances warrant it. Sometimes, you may have to throw out your day planner, your list, or your agenda. Sometimes letting go of time allows people to tap into their creativity. Continually remind yourself that time is a gift from God in which the divine purposes will be accomplished.

3. Don't Put It Off

Do you make lists of things that must be done today and feel guilty if you don't get them all done? Do you give yourself rigid deadlines for solving problems? Do you get angry with yourself when you don't come up with a solution before the deadline? Do you push yourself to get it done *now*?

Managers are conditioned to avoid procrastination, yet there are times when taking a moment to pause and regroup is all that is needed to get the creative juices flowing.

The creative process involves insight—that aha! moment, that off-the-wall idea, that sudden inspiration. Insight is the result of three steps: focus, recreate, oscillate.

First, *focus* on the task. Pour all your energy into looking at every aspect of the task in front of you. Discuss it, think about it, and define it. This is the time when you, as manager, usually call for closure and expect a solution. Instead of putting on pressure and pushing your group to do it now, move to step 2 and recreate.

Recreate means to move away from the task. Go and do something else. Get a cup of coffee. Talk about another agenda item. Tell a joke. Break for lunch. Let your subconscious mind go to work on the task.

Then try to *oscillate*, which means to switch back and forth between focusing on the task and moving away from it. Most groups tend to stick to focusing. They push to find a solution, but instead become stuck as the creative juices dry up.

Creativity flows best when you are relaxed. When the pressure is off to come up with an immediate solution, the subconscious mind goes to work. Insights occur.

The mindful manager can take time to recreate in prayer, to offer up the problem to God and wait for an answer. Many aha! moments occur after the matter has been laid aside for awhile.

4. Don't Get Emotional

Do you feel that showing your emotions in a business setting is sign of weakness? Do you try to hide your reactions when listening to other people? Do you think that keeping emotions under wrap is a sign of a strong leader? Do you feel uncomfortable when other people get emotional?

A team reacts the same way as its leader. If you keep your emotions tightly buttoned down, so will the rest of your group. You will never know how they really feel about what is happening. Your own lack of emotion will isolate you from people.

SHOWING EMOTIONS DOESN'T MEAN BEING OUT OF CONTROL. IT SIMPLY MEANS RESPONDING TO PEOPLE IN A HUMAN MANNER.

Showing emotions doesn't mean being out of control. It simply means responding to people in a human manner. If you are pleased with someone, show it. If you are angry, be open about the anger. If you are enthusiastic, let others know. When people are free to be open and human in the workplace, they are more likely to be creative. It is hard to be creative if they have to expend energy on hiding their feelings.

USING YOUR CREATIVE BRAIN

God has created wonderful, intricate, amazing human beings. You have been given a brain that can solve problems, feel emotions, sing songs, remember poetry, work out mathematical solutions, put words together, and connect with others. This wonderful God-given brain allows you to unleash your creativity at any time.

The human brain is clearly divided into two portions: the right hemisphere and the left hemisphere. Each side of the brain is used for different types of thinking:

- *Left hemisphere:* logical, sequential, intellectual, verbal, analytical, and linear
- *Right hemisphere:* creative, emotional, lateral, imaginative, intuitive, and fantastic

The way you were educated probably encouraged left-brain functions—you learned the times table, memorized the states and their capitals, and worked hard at spelling. As a result, you probably try to solve your problems with a logical, orderly approach.

Try This Exercise:

1. Imagine a huge castle on top of a mountain. A fierce storm rages around the castle. Now imagine a knight in shining armor on a big black horse galloping up the hill toward the castle. Get a strong picture of the gray skies overhead, the black horse, the silver knight. Close your eyes and hold it in your mind.
2. Slowly count to ten in your head.
3. Now, answer this question: What color is the letter S? If you have trouble with the question, keep pushing your brain to give a color to the letter S.

You probably felt jarred by the letter S question. Your brain didn't seem to be able to handle it. You may not have been able to give a color to the letter S. Here's why.

When you pictured the castle and the storm, you performed a right-brain function—you imagined something that didn't exist in your experience. Then when you counted to ten in your head, you performed a left-brain function—you remembered a sequence of numbers.

When you were asked to give the letter S a color, you were still in your left brain, the logical side, and your left brain tried to answer the question logically. Of course there is no logical answer, so you felt dislocated and uncomfortable. If you continued to push for an answer, you were faced with three choices. Your left brain, unable to process the question, relinquished it to the right brain, where you imagined a letter S and chose red, blue, green, yellow, purple, or another color. Or your left brain, determined to find an answer, simply chose the latest colors in your memory—

those of your imaginary picture—and you might have said, "Gray" (the sky), "Black" (the horse), or "Silver" (the knight). Or you may have remained stuck in your left brain and given up on the search for a color that doesn't exist.

Notice how easily you moved from your right brain (castle) to your left brain (counting). But the move from left brain (counting) to right brain (letter S color) was probably more difficult. This is true for most people. Because you were trained to use your left brain to solve problems, it is the area where you feel most comfortable. Using the right brain may be a stretch for you.

Most people have a dominant brain style—that is, they tend to use one side of their brain more than the other.

What's Your Brain Style?

Directions: Circle the number after each statement that indicates how well the statement describes you, with 5 being "very much like me" and 1 being "not at all like me."

1. I like creating options by generating lots of different ideas and thinking of lots of possible ways to do something. 1 2 3 4 5
2. I like to create order and organize. I go through stuff and eliminate the unnecessary. I like specific tasks to be assigned. 1 2 3 4 5
3. I typically have lots of materials to work with and lots of stuff around me in my work space. 1 2 3 4 5
4. I typically leave my desk and work space neat. I have a place for everything and don't begin a task until everything is tidied up from the last task. 1 2 3 4 5
5. I juggle several tasks at once. I can shift from one task to another with no problems. 1 2 3 4 5
6. I tend to have an orderly process in my work. I accomplish high-

priority things first and then move on to the lower-priority items.
1 2 3 4 5

7. I tend to go with the flow of the day, keeping my options open and being spontaneous. 1 2 3 4 5

8. I generally plan my day. I like to keep on schedule. I get annoyed by sudden changes to my schedule. 1 2 3 4 5

9. I tend to be irritated by a lot of rules, guidelines, and policies. I think they limit my ability to get things done. 1 2 3 4 5

10. For me, policies and structure keep things moving smoothly. I expect others to follow them too. 1 2 3 4 5

11. I do my best work when I'm under a tight deadline. 1 2 3 4 5

12. I am usually prompt and even early to meetings. I don't like a mad rush at the last minute. 1 2 3 4 5

13. I prefer a wide-open assignment with lots of room for my own innovations. 1 2 3 4 5

14. I'm not comfortable with a fly-by-the-seat-of-the-pants style. I think ahead and plan what I'm going to say or do. 1 2 3 4 5

15. I like a real challenge. Just tell me it can't be done, and watch me do it! 1 2 3 4 5

16. I like to follow through on things. I enjoy implementing the solution and seeing a project through to its completion. 1 2 3 4 5

17. I do my research, but I generally trust my intuition to help me do what is needed. I don't want to have too many preconceived ideas before the event. 1 2 3 4 5

18. I research all my options before going into something. In fact, planning and research are two of my strengths. 1 2 3 4 5

19. I like to move on to something new every couple of years. Once I have a job in hand, I begin to lose my enthusiasm and interest.
1 2 3 4 5

20. I like to stay with a job until I have really mastered it. In fact, I like to grow into a job and do my best work. 1 2 3 4 5

Scoring:

Add your scores for the odd-numbered questions and indicate your total here: _____

Add your scores for the even-numbered questions and indicate your total here: _____

Which is higher, the total for odd-numbered questions or even-numbered ones?

If you scored higher on the *odd-numbered* questions, you're probably right-brain dominant. This is called an *innovative* thinking style. You:

- use different ways to get results
- appear unorganized
- value the process more than the actual goal
- can be involved in more than one activity at a time

If you scored higher on the *even-numbered* questions, you're probably left-brain dominant. This is called an *adaptive* thinking style. You:

- tend to follow established patterns
- are well-organized
- focus on the goal
- are pleased when a decision is made
- prefer to work on one project at a time

If your scores are close, you probably work equally well in either hemisphere.

CREATIVITY, YOUR BRAIN, AND BRAINSTORMING

Often, when a solution eludes you or your team, brainstorming is the best approach to finding it. However, brainstorming doesn't work if you are all using the left-brain hemisphere, since creative solutions are lurking on the other side of the brain. First, try to turn off that left hemisphere. Help your brain make the shift to the right hemisphere by trying some of these techniques:

- Write with your nondominant hand for a couple of minutes.
- Put the computer mouse on the other side of the keyboard and use your other hand for a while.
- Imagine yourself lying on your favorite beach—add lots of details to your imaginary picture.
- Use aroma to shift your brain. Rose, lilac, and cinnamon are good brain shifters. Put a few drops of essential oil of rose or lilac (available at most health-food stores) on a tissue and keep it in a covered container. Lift the lid and let the aroma surround you when you feel the need to shift your brain. Or crumble a cinnamon stick and rub some of the crumbs between your fingers to release the scent.
- Listen to music. Baroque music is especially good (Pachelbel's "Canon in D" is a favorite).

Now start brainstorming. Don't number the solutions on the page. Numbering is a left-brain function, and you'll find that you will gravitate toward that number-one solution, regardless of what it is. Write your ideas all over the page—up, down, and sideways. Write down all ideas. Don't prejudge them—that's a left-brain function. Just jot them down, crazy sounding, ridiculous, or not. When no more ideas are forthcoming, leave them and go do something else for a few minutes. Then come back and evaluate, looking for the solution that will work for everyone.

If you keep thinking in the same old way, you'll arrive at the same old conclusions. It is only when you burst out of the box that you can begin to access that wonderful, creative brain God has given you. There is so much more to what happens in the synapses of your brain than you can imagine, and only when you let go of the same old way you have always done things will you begin to experience the awe and wonder of creativity.

God has given you the tools you need to do your job. It is up to you to free those tools, wipe off the rust of disuse, blow away the cobwebs of doubt and fear, and unleash the power within.

1 3

ENGAGING THE SPIRITUAL DIMENSION IN THE WORKPLACE

Your workplace is probably not very spiritual. Not everyone exhibits faith-based values and ethics. Some of your employees will lie to you. Some will cheat. Some will steal.

In your workplace, tempers can flare, voices rise in anger, and feelings get hurt. People will sulk, cry, take sides, and plot revenge.

Although your workplace may not seem like a place of blessing, it can be if you engage these four principles.

THE FOUR PRINCIPLES OF BLESSING

1. Focus on God

When you are faced with challenges in your workplace, where is the first place you look for help? Most managers focus on themselves. *Can I manage this crisis? Can I handle this person? Can I make this decision?*

If they feel they don't have the inner resources or the outer authority to deal with the issue, managers turn to a superior. *Can I take this to my boss? Is this a human resources problem? Should I call a meeting of depart-ment heads?*

As a mindful manager, get in the habit of turning to your higher power for help. In moments of crisis, take a deep breath, focus on the problem, and ask God to give you the wisdom you need to deal with the issue at hand. Your prayer doesn't have to be formal—or long. Try this exercise: breathe out through your mouth as you bring the problem or issue to God. Wait a few seconds. Then breathe in slowly through your nose, allowing your body to become still. Hold your breath as you con-sciously let the problem or issue go. Breathe out through your mouth and thank God for hearing you.

When you feel overwhelmed and stressed, focus on the God of peace.

When you feel inadequate and powerless, focus on the God of power.

When you face daily challenges that seem insurmountable, focus on the God of wisdom.

2. Feed on the Bread of Life

Each day will bring its fresh supply of challenges for you. Each challenge depletes you as you try to deal with it in an equitable manner. By the end of a tough day, you probably drag yourself out of the office, wondering if you have enough strength left to make it home. By the end of a difficult week, you are running on empty.

When God led the Israelites on their forty-year journey in the Sinai desert, God daily sent them a source of food—manna—to sustain them. The manna only lasted a day and then would spoil. They couldn't store it up for future use; they had to trust that a fresh supply would appear each day.

God has promised you sustaining soul food, offered fresh to you each day. Many believers try to keep going on the same old stale loaf. No wonder it doesn't sustain them for long. A soul-sustaining relationship with God is offered daily to you—fresh, powerful, and full of wonder.

Every day, take time to feed on things that sustain your spirit. Pray, read the scriptures or uplifting materials, meditate, and spend time with others who can encourage you. The issue isn't the amount of time you spend but the amount of food that you take in. Each day, take in enough spiritual sustenance to get you through the day. When you feel your spiritual fuel running low, give yourself a few minutes of quiet time with the divine. That may be all you need to go back into your workplace refreshed and refilled.

3. Write Down Your Goals

Someone once said that a goal not written down is just a dream. Earlier in this book, you had an opportunity to create a vision for your job. If you can, go back and re-read what that vision was. Now think of the goals you need to set in order to achieve that vision. Remember, a goal should always be SMART—specific, measurable, attainable, realistic, and timely. For example, if part of your vision is to give your employees more opportunities to learn new skills, then you can set a goal such as "organize a lunch 'n learn program every Wednesday led by other departmental personnel, starting two weeks from now." Note that the goal isn't to "get some kind of learning program in place," but was SMART.

You can do the same thing for your personal vision too.

Be sure to write down these goals. Keep yourself accountable. And expect something called "synchronicity." This is a word coined by Carl Jung that means serendipity, happenstance, or coincidence. Jung noticed that when someone makes a conscious decision, often the inner consciousness is triggered in such a way that opportunities seem to suddenly appear. You may find that someone offers to lead your lunch 'n learn program, or that a brochure arrives in the mail with a series of training programs that can be used for your staff, or that someone else has the same idea and wants to work with you.

As a mindful manager, you can call your synchronicity "God-incidence."

4. Learn to "Be"

It's easy to get caught in the workaholic trap. For one thing, it seems so commendable. People look at you with admiration and approval when you stay late to "finish up a few things." Others may think that the size of the briefcase that goes home on the weekend is indicative of your loyalty to the company.

But what is the price you pay for those extra hours of work and devotion to the job? It's a price that is measured in lost relationships, failing health, and even the risk of early death. Few people on their deathbeds wish that they had spent more time on the job. Most wish they had spent more time living—or "being."

But what is being? Being is enjoying the world at this moment—beyond the piles of paper stacked on your desk, beyond looming deadlines, beyond difficult people. Being is understanding that God has given you a life that should be lived at all levels—not just at the work level. Being is believing that there is time to savor each moment of your life—the people in it and the experiences around you. Being is living in awareness of God's love for you, to trust God to take care of all that concerns you, and to serve in the place where God has set you.

WHAT IS REQUIRED OF A MINDFUL MANAGER?

The actions you are called to as a mindful manager are contrary to the ways and expectations of the workplace. While the world says, "Anything goes as long as you don't get caught," God asks you to act justly. Not to think about justice, or to speak about justice, but to act justly. It means continually reminding yourself that every time you show fairness to those around you, you show them divine love.

In a world that spouts maxims such as, "Don't get mad, get even," the mindful manager is expected by God to love mercy. You might expect to show mercy or give mercy, but we are told to love mercy. How can you love mercy? According to *Webster's Dictionary*, mercy is "compassion or forbearance shown especially to an offender or to one subject to one's power; a blessing that is an act of divine favor or compassion; compassionate treatment of those in distress."[1] When you love mercy, these compassionate acts naturally flow from you.

> IN A WORLD THAT SPOUTS MAXIMS SUCH AS, "DON'T GET MAD, GET EVEN," THE MINDFUL MANAGER IS EXPECTED BY GOD TO LOVE MERCY.

In a world that worships upward mobility and attainment of wealth and position, the mindful manager is expected to walk humbly. You might expect God to tell you to act humbly, but the verb is *walk*. When you are walking, you are not standing still. You are moving, active, going toward something. To walk humbly with God is to give yourself completely, trusting that the paths on which you are led are part of God's plan for you. It is not waiting for God to move you but moving yourself in the direction you believe is right for you. It is believing that God will guide you, correct you, and keep you moving in the right direction.

What is required of you? These three things will lead you to the place of mindfulness that you seek: act justly, love mercy, and walk humbly.

You Are Never Alone

As you work toward becoming a mindful manager, you'll find there are still times when it seems as if God isn't there and you feel alone in your daily challenges. It is easy to move away from a position of mindfulness. So many other things intrude on your life: not just your work challenges but also your home concerns, not to mention finances, health, and security issues. Sometimes it may feel as if you take two steps back for every mindful step forward.

To bring yourself back to that place of mindfulness, focus on the Mindful Manager's Credo (page 211). You can copy this credo and keep it in your briefcase, on your desk, or in your car. Whenever you feel a sense of distance from God beginning, read through the credo prayerfully, reminding yourself that you are never alone and that God cares for you in every aspect of your life.

Being a mindful manager is a daily discipline. Like all disciplines, the more you practice the presence of God in your workplace, the easier it will be. From allowing yourself to trust in God's care, to giving your daily grind into God's keeping, you will discover a sense of inner peace that comes with your mindfulness. Within that peace you will begin to speak, act, and think with confidence as you go about your daily managerial duties. That same peace allows you to live your life fully—not just living to work, or even working to live, but seeing work as just a part of the whole life that is yours. Mindful managers know that it is possible to bring the substance of their faith into the reality of their workplace.

The Mindful Manager's Credo

I believe that God has a place in my working life.

I believe my vision for my workplace is part of God's plan.

I believe that any power I have comes from God.

I believe that stress and conflict are opportunities for me to reflect God's love to others.

I believe that my only security in a changing world lies in the unchanging nature of God.

I believe that now, this moment, is all the time I need to accomplish what is before me.

I believe that praying daily for my employees can change my workplace.

I believe that God helps me to listen to others.

I believe that God is with me in the relationships in my workplace.

I believe that God gives me the grace and the love to handle conflict.

I believe that God empowers me to be a servant so that I may empower others.

I believe that by breaking free from my old ways of thinking, I free my mind to connect with God in new ways.

I believe that to act justly, love mercy, and walk humbly are the keys to being a mindful manager.

NOTES

CHAPTER 2

1. R. L. Garner, "Humor in Pedagogy: How Ha-Ha Can Lead to Aha! (Physiological and Psychological Effects)," *College Teaching* 54, no. 1 (January 2006): 177–80.

2. Lee Berk et al., "Neuroendocrine and Stress Hormone Changes During Mirthful Laughter," *The American Journal of Medical Sciences* 298, no. 6 (December 1989): 390–96. Norman Cousins, when diagnosed with a progressive degenerative disease, explored the theory that laughter boosts the immune system. See Norman Cousins, *Anatomy of an Illness as Perceived by the Patient: Reflections on Healing and Regeneration* (New York: W.W. Norton & Co., 1979). Also, Herbert Lefcourt, a noted psychologist from the University of Waterloo in Canada, explored the possibility that a sense of humor and its use can change our emotional response to stress. See H. M. Lefcourt, *Humor and Life Stress* (New York: Springer-Verlag, 1986).

Chapter 5

1. Jennifer Tanaka, "Drowning in Data: Feeling Overwhelmed by Information? It's Time to Get Rid of Some Gadgets," *Newsweek* 129, no. 17 (April 28, 1997): 85.

2. Henry F. Lyte, "Abide with Me," *The United Methodist Hymnal* (Nashville, TN: United Methodist Publishing House, 1989), no. 700.

Chapter 9

1. See Albert Mehrabian, *Silent Messages: Implicit Communication of Emotions and Attitudes*, 2nd ed. (Belmont, CA: Wadsworth, 1981).

2. See Edward T. Hall, *The Hidden Dimension* (Garden City, NY: Anchor Books, 1982), 119–24.

Chapter 10

1. Daniel Goleman, *Emotional Intelligence: Why It Can Matter More Than IQ* (New York: Bantam Books, 1995).

Chapter 13

1. *Merriam-Webster's Collegiate Dictionary*, 11th ed., s.v. "mercy."

ABOUT THE AUTHOR

Patricia Wilson has been executive director of her own company, Life Track, for the past twenty years. The company has provided training for both secular and Christian groups, and Patricia has conducted more than one hundred business seminars across Canada and the United States annually. Now retired from the international professional-speaker circuit, she still conducts seminars and workshops for various groups and churches. She devotes most of her time to writing. She is also author of *Quiet Spaces: Prayer Interludes for Women* and *When You Come Unglued . . . Stick Close to God*. Patricia and her husband, Gerald, have three grown children and live in Nova Scotia.

Don't Miss These Books by Patricia Wilson

When You Come Unglued . . . Stick Close to God
With her folksy wisdom, Patricia Wilson shows us how to dump our baggage, resist stress, loosen up, and begin simply to be the unique individuals God created us to be. Wilson offers stimulating exercises and journal assignments such as making a gratitude list or interacting with the passengers on our "life bus." Part motivational writer, part spiritual director, part Everywoman, Wilson offers a wise and lighthearted take on the serious business of spiritual growth.
144 pages

ISBN 978-0-8358-9918-5

Quiet Spaces:
Prayer Interludes for Women
Patricia Wilson shows how you can use even a few stray minutes to calm your mind and connect with God. Each prayer interlude in *Quiet Spaces* will help refresh your spirit and give you the interlude of rest and time with God that your soul desires.
226 pages

ISBN 0-8358-0969-2

Available from your local bookstore
online at www.upperroom.org
or by phone: 1-800-972-0433

More
FRESH AIR BOOKS®

Compassion:
Thoughts on Cultivating a Good Heart
Enhance your capacity to care by cultivating a compassionate heart. Chances are, someone you know could use a little of your time, a bit of your spirit. In this little book, several writers talk about how to adopt compassion as a way of life.
96 pages

ISBN 978-0-8358-9955-0

Forgiveness: Perspectives on Making Peace with Your Past
Go beyond forgiving and forgetting. Learn how to make peace with your past. The writers in this collection say forgiving does not require you to pretend you were never hurt. It does mean finding out how to heal the past in order to embrace the future.
96 pages

ISBN 978-0-8358-9956-7

**Talk That Matters:
30 Days to Better Relationships**
Your relationships can improve
significantly when you know how to
speak with and listen to people better!
Discover ways to make meaningful
conversation possible. Short, practical
"lessons" lead you to real change.
160 pages

ISBN 978-1-935205-03-6

The Chocolated-Covered Umbrella:
Discovering Your Dreamcode

Psychotherapist Tilda Norberg explains a
simple, holistic, and enjoyable way to let
dreams speak to you. The process is not
intended as therapy but as a way to explore
what your dreams are telling you. You can
open yourself to the Holy One in a new way
that leads to spiritual discovery.
160 pages

ISBN 978-1-935205-02-9

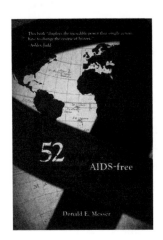